A Sanctuary for the Rights of Mankind

A SANCTUARY
for the
RIGHTS *of* MANKIND

The Founding Fathers and the Temple of Liberty

A COLUMBIAN HISTORY OF THE UNITED STATES
Book One

RICK SPAULDING *&* MAURICE YORK

WRIGHTWOOD PRESS
CHICAGO • RALEIGH

Copyright © 2008 by Rick Spaulding

Wrightwood Press
PO Box 14702, Chicago, IL 60614-0702
www.wrightwoodpress.org

Image acknowledgements: "The Apotheosis of Washington," "Honor to Washington," "America, with Peace and Freedom Blest!", "Behold! a fabric now to freedom rear'd," and "The Peace of Ghent 1814 and Triumph of America" are reprinted courtesy of the Library of Congress, Prints and Photographs Division. "Plan of the City of Washington" [L'Enfant, 1792] is reprinted courtesy of the Library of Congress, Geography and Map Division. "Mall, Map, 1928" [Andrew Jackson Downing's diagram of the Mall] is reprinted courtesy of the Frances Loeb Library, Graduate School of Design, Harvard University. "The Republic" is reprinted from *The Dream City: a portfolio of views of the World's Columbian Exposition*. N.D. Thompson Co., St Louis: 1894. The photograph of the Boston Monument and the Diagram of the Temple of Liberty are copyright Maurice York, 2008. Cover painting: John Trumbull, *Surrender of Lord Cornwallis*, 1820; courtesy of the Architect of the Capitol.

This book is registered under the Founder's Copyright
provided through Creative Commons
http://creativecommons.org/projects/founderscopyright/
All rights reserved for a period of 14 years from the date of publication, renewable for another 14 years at the option of the Wrightwood Press.

THIS WORK WILL ENTER INTO THE PUBLIC DOMAIN
BY NOVEMBER 2037

NON-PROFITS, LIBRARIES, EDUCATIONAL INSTITUTIONS,
WORKSHOP SPONSORS, STUDY GROUPS, ETC.
Special discounts and bulk purchases are available.
Please email sales@wrightwoodpress.org for more information.
You are welcome to reproduce and use any part of this work, up to 25%, for non-profit personal or group study in print or electronic form, including electronic reserves. For inquiries about use in excess of 25%, or for commercial use or re-publication, please email permissions@wrightwoodpress.org

ISBN 978-0-9801190-2-2

To freedom, to strength, to poems, to personal greatness, America is never permitted to rest, not a generation or part of a generation. To be ripe beyond further increase is to prepare to die. The architects of These States laid their foundations, and passed to further spheres. What they laid is a work done; as much more remains. Now are needed other architects, whose duty is not less difficult, but perhaps more difficult. Each age forever needs architects. America is not finished, perhaps never will be; now America is a divine true sketch.

—*Walt Whitman*

Contents

---
introduction
---
iii

---
chapter one

THE ABUSES OF KING GEORGE III

3

---
chapter two

THE PROPHECY OF PHILLIS WHEATLEY

18

---
chapter three

THE REVOLUTIONARY WAR

34

---
chapter four

BENJAMIN FRANKLIN

51

---
chapter five

THE CONSTITUTION OF THE UNITED STATES OF AMERICA

65

---
chapter six

THE FEDERALISTS

80

chapter seven

THE DEMOCRATS

94

chapter eight

THE TEMPLE OF LIBERTY

116

appendix

"TO HIS EXCELLENCY GENERAL WASHINGTON"

137

List of Illustrations

Boston Massacre Monument, Boston Common	9
"The Apotheosis of Washington"	23
"Honor to Washington"	63
"America, with Peace and Freedom Blest!"	73
"Behold! a fabric now to freedom rear'd"	74
Plan of the City of Washington	77
"Peace of Ghent 1814 and Triumph of America"	111
Andrew Jackson Downing's diagram of the Mall	122
"The Republic"	123
Diagram of the Temple of Liberty	132

Introduction

A RENEWED INTEREST IN THE FOUNDING FATHERS HAS BROUGHT forth a series of biographies about the leaders of the Revolutionary War. Joseph Ellis in *American Sphinx: The Character of Thomas Jefferson* and in *His Excellency George Washington*, David McCullough in *John Adams*, and Walter Isaacson in *Benjamin Franklin: An American Life*, have delved into a trove of primary sources and documents to present the world-historic accomplishments of these American heroes within the rich and turbulent context of their times. These new biographies, by giving a generally positive assessment of character and portraying these architects of the Republic in the light of their nobility and virtues, have excited the reading public to a revived appreciation for their greatness.

Historians and biographers of the Revolutionary War and the subsequent Founding of the United States, while striving to achieve that insight into character that is one of their principal goals, yet recognized the limitations of their studies and suggested that certain difficulties had not been fully surmounted. One basic problem that frustrated them was the question of the influence that Freemasonic lodges had on the moral and ethical development of their subjects. Generally, the secrecy enveloping these lodges prevented access to the very source documents needed by the historian, or placed those that were available in a questionable light. While this problem did not extend to Ben Franklin, who was a publicly avowed Mason and even included the path of virtue that he practiced in his *Autobiography*, it did make the evaluation of the character of the other Founders somewhat tentative and partial. Expanding the field of view outwards to encompass the whole cultural background of the political movement spearheaded by the Founders, a wealth of contextual evidence springs to life, augmenting the documents of record and illustrating a more complete landscape. The Founders' contemporaries inaugurated an outpouring of poems, music, art, sculpture, and architecture, most of it in the Neoclassic style, that embodied the social and political identity of the young nation and articulated its highest ideals. This tide of artistic expression continued into the nineteenth century, finding outlet in some of the most well-known poets and artists of the time, as well as in scores of artists whose names are forgotten today.

A strong and recurring motif of these works of art was the Spirit of Liberty, the national spirit that bound the Founders together and gave their individual struggles and ordeals a common purpose. This spirit was called by various names: sometimes Liberty, as in the Sons of Liberty or the Statue of Liberty; other times Independence, as in the Declaration of Independence; and even Columbia, as in the City of Washington, the District of Columbia. She appeared in hundreds of poems and paintings, inspired His Excellency in particular, and granted the band of brothers guidance in attaining her high purposes. The goddess with the flowing hair, carrying her staff and liberty cap, often attended by an eagle, had a ubiquitous presence. Her image graced all of the coinage of the new nation, and the national anthem invoked her name. The renewed enthusiasm in the present day for discerning the intentions of the those heroes who founded the United States of America, such evidence seems to suggest, would require a recognition of an inspiring spirit, an acknowledgement of something once very much present in the national consciousness, but now forgotten.

A second motif of such Neoclassical art, one closely connected with the Spirit of America herself, has also faded from awareness in the present day. Neoclassic artists often depicted the abode of Liberty. They envisioned her as an Indian princess or as a Greek goddess and called her dwelling place the Temple of Liberty. It was a temple built of thought and ideals, not just stone and mortar. The Freemasons, by heritage, were temple builders, craftsmen dedicated to investing architectural structures with a spiritual significance, providing both an object for contemplative reflection and a home for people actively committed to those ideals. Washington and Jefferson were both devoted to the task of constructing a building that stood as a physical expression and outward sign of the principles that had founded the nation and the inspiring spirit whom they served— a Temple of Liberty, as the Capitol building is called to this day. The Constitution itself, the document that founded the United States, was but the preamble to the founding of a temple that would bring its tenets to life. The authors of the present book hope that such an approach to the enigma of the Founding Fathers might raise to consciousness this long lost knowledge and give hope to those many Americans who seek a new direction for this country, one in accord with the intentions of her Founders.

chapter one

THE ABUSES OF KING GEORGE III

By the middle of the 18th century, the American colonies served as an economic engine for their mother country across the distant sea. Fertile, rich in natural resources, and possessing an industrious people, the colonies were a shining jewel in the extensive empire of George III, one of the richest properties in his dominion, though many considered it a cultural backwater. Sworn subjects of the King, the colonists themselves had claimed a certain measure of self-rule, convening their own popular assemblies to pass laws and govern the daily routine of civic life. Parliament, the King, his ministers, were months away by ship across the rolling waves. Yet the economic policy of England placed her colonies in a subservient position. Mercantilism favored English merchants and required the American colonists to purchase goods only from England and send their harvests and raw materials solely to English markets, to be reshipped to America in British vessels. Parliament passed various laws to insure that the American colonies followed the mercantilist policy. The hatter, who could so easily obtain fur, was not allowed to sell his hats abroad. No manufacturer was permitted to have more than two apprentices, and the making of iron was prohibited. Even the forests of

Maine were claimed by the King. His representative had the pick of trees suitable for masts in the King's navy.

Rather than pay the exorbitant prices demanded by the English merchants, the American colonists resorted to smuggling and became frugal. Especially the colonists of New England, whose manufacturing and trade were pinched and constrained, agreed to deprive themselves of luxuries and buy only necessities. Families made their own clothes from wool and flax, called "homespun." Economic associations sprang up. In the same year that three hundred young women met on Boston Common and spent the day spinning flax, the graduating class of Harvard College attended Commencement exercises clad in homespun.

By the 1750s, France had emerged as Great Britain's chief rival. The two great powers fought the Great War for the Empire, or the Seven Years War, in battles around the globe, in the far-flung provinces and colonies of the imperial rivals, and on the European continent itself. In America, the epic contest took the name of the French and Indian War. Competing claims to trapping grounds and trade routes west of the Appalachian Mountains gave rise to armed conflict that spread throughout the frontier. With the expenses of waging a multi-theater war mounting and the royal treasury rapidly depleting, England planned to defray the war's cost by taxing her American colonies and prepared to insure the compliance of the colonial assemblies by a stricter enforcement of the navigation laws, which governed the types of ships and goods that could enter American ports. To that end, Parliament authorized the extensive use of general search warrants, or "Writs of Assistance." First implemented under Charles II, they allowed customs officials to enter any home, warehouse, or ship in search of smuggled goods. Customhouse officials, search warrants in hand, were free to go wherever they pleased, backed by the local sheriff or constable. Boston merchants, outraged by the unjust treatment of subjects of the Crown, finally brought a case against the Custom Commissioner, Charles Paxton, in the winter of 1760. John Adams watched, a spectator to a test of the Crown's ability to do as it pleased in the colonies, as Mr. Gridley, his mentor, supported the Writs and argued in favor of their use, while James Otis, his idol, defended the resistance of the American merchants. The effect of this trial on Adams was enormous. He attended the entire proceeding, and in a letter he told of experiencing an abyss opening at this feet and a veil being rent as he experienced a revelation of the spiritual background of this confrontation: that behind the figure of Gridley stood the spirit of Great Britain and behind Otis, the youthful spirit of America. Watching this mighty struggle unfold in the confines of a cramped courtroom, Adams jotted a careful observation that would ring with significance for the coming struggles: "the child, Independence, was born."

In 1765 Parliament, led by George Grenville and urged on by the King, passed a bill in an effort to raise money by taxing the American colonists on all papers distributed to the public, both official and popular, including newspapers, almanacs, legal papers, and pamphlets. The colonists took up the rallying cry coined by Otis soon after the Paxton trial, "Taxation without representation is tyranny," and their protests against the Stamp Act shocked the British government. Incited to extend this theme into legislative resolve, Patrick Henry—a young lawyer and freshman member of the Virginia assembly—delivered one of his greatest orations against the act. On a sweltering day in April, a young Thomas Jefferson stood in the doorway of the House of Burgesses and listened to Henry's words which reached a crescendo when he exclaimed: "Caesar had his Brutus, Charles I his Cromwell, and George III…" "Treason! Treason!" shouted the speaker of the House and other friends of the crown. "…May profit by their example," Henry continued; "If that be treason, make the most of it." The inspiration of these words entered Jefferson's heart and sealed it to the cause of Independence. The New Idea of the New World, which had appeared to John Adams in a vision, now manifested in oratory and stirred the mind of Jefferson.

Henry's oratory brought this inspiration to life throughout the colonies as well. Newspaper reports of the resolution he introduced into the House of Burgesses, declaring that only the people themselves or a representative chosen by them could levy taxes, sparked the legislatures of eight more colonies to draft resolutions modeled on the one passed by Virginia. The Pennsylvania Journal summarized what was behind this unusually cohesive shout of dissent, observing that "as soon as the Spark of Patriotism began to kindle, it flew like Lightning from Breast to Breast—it flowed from every Tongue, and Pen, and Press, 'till it had diffused itself through every Part of the British Dominions in America; it united us all, we seem'd to be animated by one Spirit, and that was the Spirit of Liberty." Colonial opponents of the Stamp Act rallied in secrecy to oppose the Crown and called themselves "Sons of Liberty." Associations called by this name sprang up throughout the colonies and began to form communication channels among themselves. Within weeks of Henry's address, they threatened neither to use stamps nor permit their distribution. The resistance decorated the Liberty Tree in Boston with the effigies of friends of the British authorities, and a rioting mob swept through the city destroying property and terrorizing royal officials. This gross exercise of the power of the mob touched off spontaneous riots in other colonies, targeting royally-appointed stamp distributors. Taxes went uncollected, and the law was rendered unenforceable. The Sons of Liberty had brought Parliament's design to its knees. Merchants in the major colonial cities agreed to send no orders to England until Parliament repealed the Stamp Act. William Pitt, on the verge of retirement, and a young Edmund Burke seconded their demands for repeal, and Benjamin Franklin joined the chorus when the House of Commons asked to hear the American position. The consequent repeal of this hated Act brought rejoicing in the American colonies. Statues to Pitt were erected in New York, Virginia and Maryland.

The struggle between Great Britain and its American colonies took a more violent turn in 1770. Charles Townsend led a renewed attempt in Parliament to tax the American colonies. The Townsend Acts imposed new duties on imported goods and relied on expanded use of warrantless searches under the Writs of Assistance to tighten the vise on smuggled goods, which circumvented the tax. The Sons of Liberty rose to action once again, spreading a boycott of imports and blockading British ships with their own vessels. Determined that the Acts should succeed, goaded to action at each step by King George

III, Townsend sent British warships as a stern warning to the colonies to cooperate with the imposed taxes. A British man-of-war, the *Romney*, arrived in Boston harbor and proceeded to board New England ships and impress their seamen. John Hancock's sloop, the *Liberty*, was seized. In response to further outbreaks of violence against customs officials, General Gage brought a regiment of Redcoats to Boston. Gage posted sentinels on the street corners, and Boston became a conquered town. Friction between the citizens and soldiers mounted until it exploded in blood and misery in a crowded alleyway. The outraged citizenry demanded that the sailors of the *Pitt* who were responsible for the deaths of five Bostonians—the great Boston Massacre—be put on trial. John Adams astounded his fellow citizens by stepping forward to take the principal lead in the trial as the defense attorney of Captain Preston. Even more unsettling to those who demanded vengeance for the blood spilt that day, Adams won the Captain's acquittal, along with five of the seven other British sailors involved in the shooting. He showed in court how the unruly mob, by cornering the sailors in an alley and threatening them with clubs and stones, was the real culprit, exonerating the captain, who had not ordered the sailors to fire, as well as the sailors, whose fear of bodily harm had prompted their wrongful actions. Accepting the hatred that would descend on his head from friends and supporters of the colonial cause, even his fellow Sons of Liberty, Adams followed the dictates of his conscience. Sensible that he was placing his very life on the line, Adams later wrote that he had "devoted myself to endless labour and Anxiety if not to infamy and death, and that for nothing, except, what indeed was and ought to be all in all, sense

The Abuses of King George III

Boston Massacre Monument, Boston Common. (Bronze, Robert Kraus, 1888)

of duty." He had witnessed the sinister and disturbing underbelly of popular opposition to the Stamp Act, and he now stood in opposition to mob action, showing England that at least some Bostonians were motivated by principles of justice. He protected his ideal, the child Independence, from the danger of mob rule, though her seeming friends would have led her into it. Even as he had seen the deeper significance of the trial over the Writs of Assistance, Adams grasped the momentous event that stood just beyond the chaos and violence of that day—one hidden from the citizens of Boston in the haze of vengeance, but later commemorated in the memorial to the Massacre that still stands on Boston Common: the Spirit of America, her great eagle at her side, a newly-broken chain upraised in one hand, the Crown crushed under her foot.

Finally Parliament agreed to forego further efforts to wring funds from the colonies to offset the high costs of the late war and the ongoing defense of its colonies. It repealed the Townsend Duties and left only a three-penny tax on tea as emblematic of its right to raise revenue from the colonies without the prior consent of the colonial assemblies. The tension between the colonial position and that of the crown eased, and a return to normal relations seemed possible. Yet in 1773, Parliament compounded its mismanagement of American affairs by passing a measure to help out the financially ailing British East India Company. The act allowed the company to dump their tea in America at prices so low that colonial merchants could not compete. Certain patriotic citizens seized on this slight by Parliament and stirred the drink of war with the straw of humor. They dressed in Native American garb and turned Boston Harbor into a gigantic teapot. Paul Revere carried the news to New York and Philadelphia, provoking similar actions throughout the colonies. Parliament, now directed by Lord North, took the Boston Tea party as a personal affront and passed a series of Acts that closed the port of Boston, placed the government of the colony directly under the King's control, and allowed royal officials accused of criminal actions to have their trials moved to other colonies or even to Great Britain. Four regiments of Redcoats arrived in Boston, demanded quarters of its citizens, and closed the port.

All of Boston was plunged into great distress. Many citizens depended on commerce for their daily bread, and families suffered. Other colonies came to their aid: South Carolina sent two hundred barrels of rice and promised more, North Carolina raised two thousand pounds by subscription, Philadelphia four thousand pounds, and Virginia also raised money and sent over one hundred barrels of flour. Even the citizens of Quebec donated a thousand bushels of wheat, while London subscribed a vast sum of money. This outpouring of support stiffened the citizens' resolve. General Gage, Commander-in-chief of the British army and newly-appointed governor of Massachusetts, forbade meetings to discuss public affairs. The leaders of Boston held them anyway, and when Fanueil Hall proved too small for their gathering, the assemblage swarmed to the Old South Church. Someone hoisted a flag in the Liberty Tree, and processions of the popular movement saluted it as they passed by.

The neighboring colonies were not directly impacted by the Intolerable Acts or by the actions of the army against Boston, but sympathy with the plight of their brethren in Massachusetts ran deep. Concern over the tactics employed by Parliament and its agents grew into a fear that if the crown could alter the Massachusetts charter without consultation or approbation, it could very well do the same to all of them. So-called committees of correspondence in every county, parish, and township passed word of the Boston port closure and the outrages practiced on its citizens. Throughout the colonies conventions assembled and chose delegates to gather for a general meeting to debate whether and how the colonies should make common cause with Massachusetts in order to prevent future abuses against them all. The meeting would become the First Continental Congress. Only Georgia lacked representation when the fifty-five delegates came together in Philadelphia. Patrick Henry arose to speak first. He breathed fire into the assembled representatives as he had done so many times before. John Adams, who attended the Congress and took notes on all that was said each day, listened as Patrick Henry declared that "the present state of things show that government is dissolved." "The distinctions between Virginians, Pennsylvanians, New Yorkers, and New Englanders, are no more," he thundered; "I am not a Virginian, but an American." Though Henry argued for the Congress to institute a new form of government for the one that he saw as fallen, the moderates carried the day. The Congress instituted a boycott on British imports, addressed a list of grievances to the king, and agreed to convene again in the spring.

As the cold days of winter began to retreat the following March, they drew up the veil on ever-heightening tensions between the citizens of Massachusetts and the army camped on their doorstep, indeed, in their living rooms. In the villages and towns around Boston, the colonial militia gathered and carried out military exercises. General Gage concluded that suppression of the insurgency required a show of force and the capture of stores of munitions being laid up in surrounding townships. Hoping for a bloodless sortie into the countryside, Gage wished to move with all the stealth and speed he could muster. On the eighteenth of April, 1775, in the wee hours of the morning, a force of fifteen hundred Redcoats began the nineteen mile march to Concord by way of Lexington. The Sons of Liberty took to their horses and spread the alarm to farm and village as the Minutemen fell to arms. A skirmish broke out on Lexington Green and several colonials died before their line melted away into houses and woods, and the Redcoats pressed on to Concord. Rather than a fully-stocked arsenal and supply depot, the

British discovered only two small cannons for their trouble. Pursuing the town militia, which withdrew to high ground on the north end of Concord to await reinforcements, three companies of the expeditionary force reached the bridge over the Concord River. Joseph Emerson, grandfather of Ralph Waldo Emerson and future Chaplin of the Continental Army, watched from his porch as the patriot farmers stood their ground and "fired the shot heard round the world." Longfellow later immortalized the deeds of the Minutemen in "The Midnight Ride of Paul Revere," and one hundred years after the event Daniel Chester French commemorated the victory at the bridge with the Minuteman Statue. During the retreat to Boston, the British force was decimated. Shots fired from behind hedges and trees struck private and officer alike. The Redcoats suffered nearly three hundred casualties.

In Philadelphia, the Liberty Bell pealed its praise of the battles at Lexington and Concord. Just three weeks later, on the tenth of May, the Second Continental Congress, with John Hancock as its president, convened in the State House. The delegates assumed authority, provided for a standing army, and took the decisive measure of appointing George Washington as Commander-in-chief. On June 17, 1775, General Gage ordered a second assault on the rebels, one directed at Breed's Hill. As John Adams debated with his fellow delegates in Carpenter's hall, his wife Abigail heard the roar of gun and canon fire from their farm in Braintree. Clad in homespun and armed with every manner of firearm they could bring to hand, the Minutemen solemnly took up the call of Patrick Henry to "give me liberty or give me death." With Putman exhorting his men to "not fire till you see the whites of their eyes," the patriot militia fended off two charges before withdrawing in the face of a superior British force. The American force lost over four hundred men; the British more than one thousand. The Revolutionary War had begun.

As revolutionary feeling stirred with the start of armed conflict, Thomas Paine, an Englishman whom Benjamin Franklin had encouraged to emigrate to America, was working as editor of Franklin's magazine, *The Pennsylvania Gazette*. He published *Common Sense* in January, 1776, just at the moment when the outrageous impositions of Parliament and the spilt blood in Massachusetts had proven to the colonists that there could be no reconciliation with Britain. It became an instant best-seller, the Northern counterpart of Henry's stirring orations. Historians often call it the efficient cause of the Revolutionary War since it set the colonists in motion to rise up against the King. Up until this time the Sons of Liberty had held their quarrel with Parliament, claiming their rights under the Crown as "loyal subjects" of King George III and demanding equal treatment as British citizens. Paine's pamphlet stripped the crown of its pretensions and trampled on the divine right of kings, its theological underpinning. Paine argued that the King held equal, if not greater responsibility, for the abuses since he had supported Parliament. Paine confronted his countrymen with the fundamental problem of their identity as Englishmen: were they bound by loyalty to the King and forced to capitulate simply because of the King's divine and established right, or were they to assert their rights according to their own conscience. The great irony of Paine's argument was that, since the time of the

Stamp Act, the King had suffered from a mysterious illness that put the question more bluntly: should the American colonists give their loyalty to a man who was going insane? Decades after the revolutionaries accomplished their goal, Emerson presented Paine's argument in perhaps its most felicitous form in his essay, "Self-reliance":

> "The world has indeed been instructed by its kings, who have so magnetized the eyes of nations. It has been taught by this colossal symbol the mutual reverence that is due from man to man. The joyful loyalty with which men have everywhere suffered the king, the noble, or the great proprietor to walk among them by a law of his own, make his own scale of men and things, and reverse theirs, pay for benefits, not with money but with honor, and represent the Law in his person, was the hieroglyphic by which they obscurely signified their consciousness of their own right and comeliness, the right of every man."

The common sense of the colonists told them that the principle of kingship dwelt in the soul of each human being. History now demanded the elevation of the common man to his rightful position.

When the Second Continental Congress reassembled in 1776, it chose a committee to voice its opposition to King George III. The committee, which included John Adams and Ben Franklin, assigned Jefferson the task of stating the charges which warranted formal separation of America from Great Britain. Jefferson listed the attacks of the crown on the democratic institutions of America and showed the abuses of the King to be the actions of a tyrant directed against the spirit of liberty residing in the town meetings of the North and the chambers of the House of Burgesses in the South. The Second Continental Congress revised Jefferson's draft of the Declaration of Independence, but instructed that its original wording be preserved and that a proper reproduction of this masterpiece include their changes in the margin. Jefferson achieved fame for his deed and the title of "Pen of the Revolution." His mastery of the Neoclassic style was only matched by the political content therein. Such unity of form and content points to the presence of an inspiring spirit who stands behind all such achievements belonging to the realms of gold. The spirit, whom Adams had called Independence, possessed Jefferson and infused every statement of the Declaration of Independence.

Walt Whitman believed, like Herder, that great poetry is always the result of a national spirit. The spirit of America had spoken through the orations of James Otis and Patrick Henry to awake John Adams and Thomas Jefferson and other Sons of Liberty to the cause of freedom. It had recently addressed the American people through Paine's essay and had won them over to the side of freedom by exposing the folly of delaying formal separation from England. With the adoption of the Declaration of Independence, this spirit addressed the world. Bells tolled throughout the city of Philadelphia, and the crowd that had gathered for the event erupted with shouts of joy. The Declaration was published and read to the Continental Army, inspiring its audience then as it has continued to do down to the present day. Independence, that child envisioned by Adams sixteen years earlier, intoned the self-evident truths of reason. The Spirit of

Liberty, who had stood behind the actions of her sons, who had enlivened tree and bell for her followers, now declared the causes for separation. On July 4, 1776, Liberty stepped onto the stage of world history and founded a new nation, the United States of America.

chapter two

THE PROPHECY OF PHILLIS WHEATLEY

The Second Continental Congress chose George Washington as the Commander-in-chief of the Continental Army in no small part to placate the Southern delegates. His nomination to the post came from John Adams, acting as delegate to the Congress from Massachusetts. Washington's claim to such a great responsibility involved a most unlikely series of events. During the French and Indian War, he had joined the military effort of the colonies as they proudly fought in support of the Crown. Washington had been a member of the Virginia militia less than a year when Governor Dinwiddie sent the young Major to deliver an ultimatum to the French. Washington undertook the long journey over difficult terrain in adverse weather, only to be rebuffed by the French commander at Fort Le Boeuf and faced with an untimely near demise as he was fired on at point-blank range during his return. The following year, in 1754, Washington led a force of over a hundred men to try to establish a strategic fort at the confluence of the Monongahela, the Ohio, and the Allegheny rivers. A much larger French force was already constructing Fort Duquesne there, and their attack on Washington's hastily built

Fort Necessity compelled his surrender. Despite having killed a number of French soldiers in an earlier skirmish, Washington and his soldiers,—less two officers kept as hostages by the French,—were allowed to report back to Dinwiddie with a demand for surrender. A third expedition to the present site of Pittsburg began in May of 1755, although in this instance Washington served as an aide of General Braddock, who led a British army of two thousand men in an effort to drive the French out of the Ohio River Valley. Washington took sick on the journey and lay in bed as French soldiers and their Native American allies ambushed the British vanguard, killing almost nine hundred Redcoats and most of their officers, including General Braddock himself. Washington joined the fray and took command of the disoriented and helpless soldiers, ordering a retreat that saved at least a remnant from complete disaster. Two horses were shot from under him, and he later discovered bullet holes in his shirt and hat. Miraculously, he walked away unscathed.

Washington's leadership manifested in the midst of General Braddock's debacle. He attained the rank of colonel in the Virginia militia at age twenty-three, and the Virginia governor placed him in charge of the defense of the western border, a hopeless task considering the hit-and-run tactics of the Native-American allies of the French. With the end of the French and Indian War, Washington traded his commission for the role of Virginia planter until the opening of hostilities with Britain and the imperial army in which he had formerly served. Despite the fact that he had been out of military service for fifteen years and that many candidates for the position of commander-in-chief had far more experience, the Second Continental Congress unanimously selected Washington to lead the Continental Army. He took command of the patriot army outside of Boston on July 2, 1775, and shouldered the seemingly impossible burden of opposing the greatest military force in the world. It was the twenty-first anniversary of his defeat at Fort Necessity.

Thomas Paine published a poem in the April, 1776, issue of the *Pennsylvania Gazette* in the hope that it might instill confidence in those Americans whose support for the revolution was wavering. The poem, "To His Excellency, General Washington," celebrated Washington's appointment as Commander-in-chief of the Continental Army. The young, black woman who had written it was unknown to Americans, although audiences in England had appreciated her poetry and had even raised money by subscription to purchase her freedom from bondage. Phillis Wheatley's poem to Washington accomplished Paine's intention. More than simply extolling the General, Wheatley's poem gave a name to the inspiration that was uniting and driving the colonies on towards independence. Her poem began by giving the guiding spirit of America, (whom Adams had called Independence,) the appellation of Columbia. It proceeded to describe her in Neo-classic terms:

> The goddess comes, she moves divinely fair,
> Olive and laurel binds her golden hair:
> Whenever shines this native of the skies,
> Unnumber'd charms and recent graces rise.

The poem next presented a prophecy of the impending struggle between Columbia and Britannia, that spirit of England once glimpsed by Adams during the trial over the Writs of Assistance. It told of the climax of their war when the scales of Libra, held aloft by Jupiter, would show the side of Britannia sinking down and the British invasion being crushed. Her poem concluded with a vision of the honors that Washington would receive as a consequence of remaining faithfully in her service. His countrymen and the heavenly realm alike would commemorate his service to Columbia.

Phillis Wheatley sent her poem and a letter to General Washington in October of 1775. He sent her a reply the following February, inviting her to come to Cambridge and visit him at the command post of the Continental Army. In the letter he also apologized for his tardy response and explained his unwillingness to assist her in publishing her poem owing to a personal abhorrence of vanity. Wheatley then resided in Providence, Rhode Island, in the home of her good friend, the daughter of her former owner. They had fled Boston together because of the British occupation, but with the withdrawal of the British army, Wheatley was able to return to her home in Boston in March of 1776 and travel thence to Cambridge to meet with Washington. No tale has been told of their meeting. It seems likely that the general might have asked the poetess to recite her poem for him. Although this poem is usually called a panegyric, it is properly a plea and a challenge to Washington to submit to Columbia's guidance, a warning that the general might more have taken to heart had he heard such an oracle spoken by the poetess herself:

> Proceed, great chief, with virtue on thy side,
> Thy ev'ry action let the goddess guide.
> A crown, a mansion, and a throne that shine,
> With gold unfading, WASHINGTON! Be thine.

The later choice of "Hail, Columbia," written in 1798, as the national anthem of the United States of America shows the essential agreement of the Founding Fathers with Wheatley's insight. (The national anthem was changed to "The Star-Spangled Banner" in March, 1931.) The very name of the capital of America—Washington, the District of Columbia—links Columbia and her champion for all the world to see. Less well known are the hundreds of works by architects, sculptors, painters, musicians, and poets who said the same thing to smaller audiences, often adding the idea that Columbia's greatest hero was America's Hercules. The idea that Washington and Hercules were connected together possibly found its origin in the medal that Benjamin Franklin struck to commemorate the Treaty of Paris at the close of the Revolution. It placed Hercules in Washington's stead and showed the infant Hercules holding a snake in either hand, symbols of the two great victories that had sealed the outcome of the war and the birth of the new nation—one Saratoga, the other Yorktown. Over Hercules stood Liberty in the armor of Minerva, her right hand grasping a spear, her left a shield bearing the fleur-de-lis of France, with which she fended off the lion of England. The following year, in 1784, Francois painted "Allegory of the American Union," a symbolic representation of the triumph of America in the Revolutionary War. His picture showed the thirteen states as a bridge spanning a yawning chasm. The hero standing atop the bridge was Hercules. Constantine Brumidi, who had left his native Italy to come to the United States and devote his life to adorning the Capitol building, painted one of the foremost of these artistic creations. His masterpiece recalled Michelangelo's

The Prophecy of Phillis Wheatley

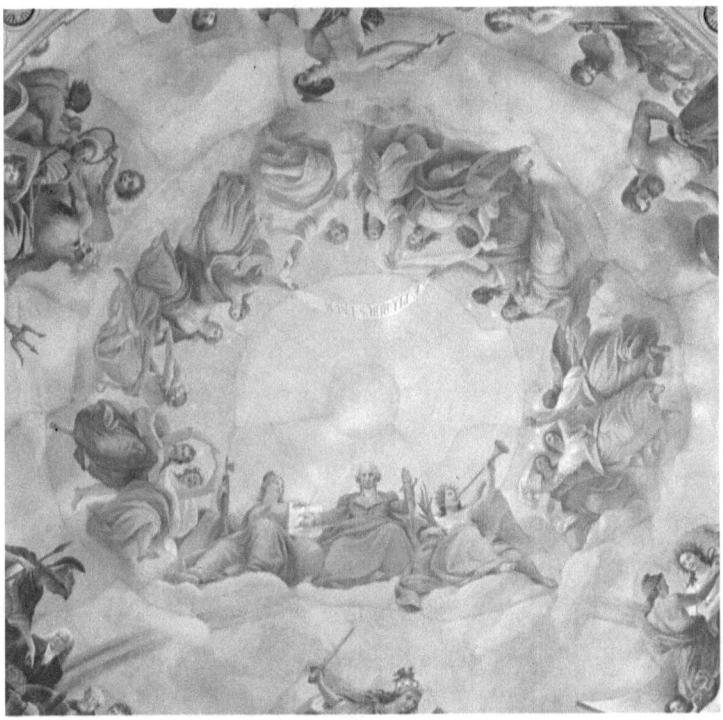

"The Apotheosis of Washington" (Fresco detail, Constantine Brumidi, 1866)

feat and covers the interior of the dome of the Capitol to this day. The fresco depicts Wheatley's prophetic vision of Washington's deification in classical iconography. "The Apotheosis of Washington" shows Washington at Columbia's side, circled by the Spirits of the thirteen colonies, looking down from the starry firmament. The painting echoes the Greek view of the apotheosis of Hercules, whose constellation is surrounded by the zodiac, symbols of his twelve labors.

Artists, historians, and politicians of the day took every opportunity to draw explicit parallels between America and the

Republic of ancient Rome. In the nobility of her heroes and in the civic virtues of her government, Rome reflected the highest ideals of the Founders. One of Shakespeare's Roman plays, *Antony and Cleopatra*, is set against the backdrop of the civil war that brought an end to five hundred years of republican government and signaled the rise of the imperial monarchy—the inverse of the events at the close of the eighteenth century, when the colonies sought to throw off the yoke of imperialism in order to establish a republican form of government. At the center of the action was the warlike dispute between Mark Antony and Octavius Caesar, two of the three members of the Second Triumvirate, who held supreme political authority within the Republic. Whereas Shakespeare generally modeled such plays on Plutarch's *Lives*, adding but a few scenes of his own in confirmation of the Greek historian's insight, in his final play in this vein he differed with Plutarch's characterization of Antony and Cleopatra. Plutarch's emphasis on the mission of Octavian to usher in the *Pax Romana*, or Roman Peace, played second fiddle in Shakespeare's play to the love of Marc Antony and the Queen of the Nile or, as some critics have called it, the theme of last love. Octavian gained the whole world, defeating his rivals and elevating himself to emperor and divinity, but Shakespeare intimated that this deed had endangered his very soul. Octavian had even used his sister as a pawn of his cunning, marrying her off to Antony on pretence of truce and friendship, but his deceit and cleverness ultimately left him alone. Antony lost the whole world, but, like Brutus in *Julius Caesar*, he had conquered himself. His love for Cleopatra was not in vain, for he had redeemed the soul of his beloved, whose wiles and stratagems melted away when she heard the declaration of his love made with his dying breath. Her new-found integrity emerged in the final act when she imitated her lover's example. She took her own life.

While drawing this contrast between Antony and Octavian, Shakespeare suggested the presence of a connection between Antony and Hercules. In Act 2, in the rising action of the play, the soothsayer delivers a warning that Antony's angel must cower before that of Octavian, saying:

> Thy daemon, that thy spirit which keeps thee, is
> Noble, courageous, high unmatchable,
> Where Caesar's is not; but near him thy angel
> Becomes afeared, as being o'erpowered.[†]

The play reaches its climax as Antony and Octavian's argument breaks into open war; as the plot moves into the falling action in Act 4, a group of soldiers gathers in camp after the fatal battle of Actium. In this corresponding event to the soothsayer's prophecy, the soldiers hear a swelling cacophony of music from under the earth.

> 3RD SOLDIER: "Peace, I say! What should this mean?
> 4TH SOLDIER: "'Tis the god Hercules, whom Antony loved, Now leaves him."[‡]

Nine scenes later, Antony himself invokes his relation with Hercules, also known as Alcides, as he discovers that Cleopatra's ships, the key to his success, have again abandoned him to defeat. Blinded by rage, he howls at his lover's betrayal:

[†] II.iii.19-22.
[‡] IV.iii.14-16.

> The shirt of Nessus is upon me. Teach me,
> Alcides, thou mine ancestor, thy rage.
> Let me lodge Lichas on the horns o' the moon,
> And with those hands that grasped the heaviest club
> Subdue my worthiest self.†

While Antony's association with Hercules can be accepted in a purely metaphorical or poetical sense (Antony is clearly not a blood descendant of Hercules), the classical literature with which Shakespeare himself was also familiar suggests a deeper, alternative reading. In the climactic event of Virgil's *Aeneid*—the founding work of ancient Rome, written to glorify none other than Octavian as Caesar Augustus—the hero Aeneas journeys to the Underworld, where he meets his dead father, Anchises. Anchises acts as Aeneas' guide, leading him through the Elyssian Fields, until they come across a great multitude waiting to leave their paradise and return to the world above.

> "But, Father, can it be that any souls
> would ever leave their dwelling here to go
> beneath the sky of earth, and once again
> take on their sluggish bodies? Are they madmen?
> Why this wild longing for the light of earth?"

Anchises turns to Aeneas and imparts to him the secret of reincarnation.

> "Son, you will have the answer; I shall not
> keep you in doubt," Anchises starts and then
> reveals to him each single thing in order....
> Therefore they are schooled by punishment
> And pay with torments for their old misdeeds:
> some there are purified by air, suspended
> and stretched before the empty winds; for some
> the stain of guilt is washed away beneath

a mighty whirlpool or consumed by fire.
First each of us must suffer his own Shade;
Then we are sent through wide Elysium—
A few of us will gain the Fields of Gladness—
until the finished cycle of the ages,
with lapse of days, annuls the ancient stain
and leaves the power of ether pure in us,
the fire of spirit simple and unsoiled.
But all the rest, when they have passed time's circle
for a millennium, are summoned by
the god to Lethe in a great assembly
that, free of memory, they may return
beneath the curve of the upper world, that they
may once again begin to wish for bodies."‡

Anchises then told his son a greater secret, that the heroes of ancient Greece had returned to earth and had taken part in the founding of the Roman Empire. Virgil viewed Octavian as the culmination of this process, the last of the great Greek heroes to reincarnate.

One of the founding legends of Greece, the epic tale of the quest for the Golden Fleece, tells the story of those heroes and their voyage on the *Argo* under Jason's leadership. Fifty heroes joined Jason on the great ship—Orpheus, the singer; Castor and Pollux, the twin brothers of Helen; Peleus, the father of Achilles; and the mighty Hercules along with his companion, Hylas—and set out to wrest the prized Fleece from the king of Colchis and the dragon he had set to guard it. While Virgil's indications draw the lines between the Greek and Roman heroes

---

† IV.xii.43-47.
‡ *The Aeneid*. Translated by Alen Mandelbaum. Bantam Classics. Book 6, pp. 156-157, lines 948-55 and 975-993.

and invite examination of their character and virtues, a comparison of the events surrounding the great quest for the Golden Fleece with those of the Roman Civil War also bears the weight of the poet's insight. Antony wilted before Octavian, a strange fate for one with the strength of Hercules; yet it was prefigured in Hercules' defeat by Jason in the rowing contest—the only contest of skill that Jason won among his companions. Hercules was greatest among the heroes and by rights should have led the quest, but when the question of leadership arose, Hercules himself nominated Jason. Later in the voyage, when Hylas was abducted at Kios, the grief-stricken Hercules abandoned the quest, leaving Jason the undisputed leader of the heroes. Octavian triumphed over Antony and achieved the golden round of kingship, just as Jason once had led the fifty heroes of Greece and accomplished the Quest of the Golden Fleece. Octavian's triumph proved to be hollow in Shakespeare's portrayal, and so was Jason's. He had won the Golden Fleece only with the aid of Medea, the princess of Colchis, who had helped him out of love. She used her knowledge and spells to defeat the tests of King Aeëtes and circumvent the dragon in exchange for his promises that he would take her away to Greece and marry her. Upon his return to Greece, Jason discovered that having a foreign bride stood in the way of receiving the approbation that he desired from his countrymen. Jason later abandoned her at Corinth to marry the king's daughter in hope of gaining the fame he sought. Medea's revenge was swift. She poisoned the king and his daughter both, then stabbed to death her own two children by Jason. In despair, Jason took his own life.

The idea of reincarnation also sheds some light on the

character of the enigmatic Queen of Egypt, whose soothsayer may have seen the threads connecting her life with that of Medea. In the 1860s, the sculptor William Wetmore Story created two sculptures in marble, one of Cleopatra and one of Medea. Cleopatra lounges on a chair, glowering into the distance, as if contemplating her abandonment by Antony, while Medea stands with knife in hand, a menacing and complex storm of anger on her face. Both women wear identical bracelets—a snake entwined about their left forearm. Like Story's two sculptures, the character of Cleopatra and Medea show strong parallels. Cleopatra's magical charms seem to reflect Medea's spells; Cleopatra's wiles, Medea's cleverness; and Cleopatra's abiding distrust of men's love, Medea's horror at her husband's treachery. The plot of Octavius Caesar to capture Cleopatra alive and put her on display for Romans to gawk at seems inexplicably cruel since Cleopatra herself had done no evil to Octavian, but it begins to gain substance as an echoing action born of the unsatisfied rage buried deep in Octavian's soul at the furious revenge Medea had taken on Jason for his betrayal. Antony's final deed—his botched suicide of falling upon his own sword after hearing of Cleopatra's death—thus gains new dimension and depth; it becomes the means of redeeming the evil destiny that had beset Cleopatra. The greatest warrior of the Roman world willingly accepted defeat and even death in order to help the Queen of the Nile rediscover the goodness and nobility that had resided in the bosom of the princess of Colchis before the arrival of the Argo.

The cliché that history repeats itself appeared in its proper form in *The Philosophy of History*, where Hegel explained that the first occurrence of a truly world historic event astounds the multitudes of people, and its repetition is necessary in order to provide proof, as it were, for the confused people who did not perceive the significance of the initial event. Hegel illustrated his concept of repetition with an example drawn from Roman history. Julius Caesar viewed himself as the man-god and ushered into the world the idea of kingship. Not until Octavian took upon himself the title of Caesar Augustus and ushered in the era of empire did this idea receive its corroboration. Hegel showed the gloomy effect of the rule of the Caesars on ancient Rome. He pointed out the fundamental truth of Brutus's insight, that the Roman people, originators of rule by law, by placing their emperor above the law, had turned all Roman citizens into slaves. Brutus' mistake, according to Hegel, was his failure to recognize that historical necessity was at work, his foolish belief that the murder of Julius Caesar could halt the inevitable subjugation of the people by a self-exalted demigod. The advance in history that Caesar Augustus represented also occurred in the Eastern world, where the idea of kingship was the central theme in the legend of the first emperor of China. Neither Brutus, by stabbing, nor Antony, by opposing, could prevent the appearance of the man-god and the *Pax Romana*. By placing his likeness on the drachma and causing the whole world to be taxed, Octavian fulfilled his mission.

  The theme of *The Philosophy of History* is the Idea of Freedom, and the concept of repetition is but one of its handmaidens. For Hegel, the turning point of history was the appearance of the god-man whose manifestation on the earthly plane began with the call for all the world to be taxed and a journey to Bethlehem by a carpenter and his wife. This event could only occur once in history since it was truly an act of freedom, not necessity, and it would send a rippling change through all that went before in much the same way that the climax of a literary masterpiece influences the rising actions of the plot and illuminates them in a new light. The full meaning of the sacrifice of the god who became man would gradually unfold in the coming centuries, but Hegel insisted that only the spirit of those human beings who are fully awake and self-conscious could be witness to its truth. Hegel characterized the initial experience of this Idea for those persons awake to its import as the dawning of the spirit of brotherhood. Love for one's fellow man flowed out of the sacrifice of the God of Love. This love foreshadowed the end of slavery, for the principle of freedom in human relationships sustains the freely-given offer of grace for all men. Antony's sacrifice, placed in this context, arises with new significance as a deed meant to redeem a single soul, that of Cleopatra.

The works of Constantine Brumidi and the myriad of other artists who pointed to a connection between George Washington and Hercules, when joined with Shakespeare's indication of the relation between Hercules and Marc Antony, helps illumine the mystery of Phillis Wheatley's prophecy—why she saw so early and so clearly, not just Washington's victory in the Revolutionary War, but his apotheosis, as it were. The first half of Wheatley's life stands as a strange reflection of the plan that Octavian had in store for Cleopatra: to place her in a cage, include her in his triumphal march, and leave her on display to the end of her days. Cleopatra's suicide foiled Octavian's immediate plan, but it may not have actually prevented this destiny from descending on her. Phillis Wheatley arrived in America at the age of seven, wearing chains. None of Boston's citizens believed that John Wheatley's slave could write poetry, nor would they pay for subscriptions or otherwise support her. Wheatley's poetic gift, which quickly and precociously emerged as she absorbed her adopted language, almost seems a metamorphosis of Cleopatra's charms in an artistic direction. The meeting of Phillis Wheatley with George Washington in Cambridge proved to be the climax of her life. In one sense it was her opportunity to escape the evil destiny that had befallen her, since having a patron such as Washington would certainly soften the negative view that Bostonians held of her. In a deeper sense, though, Wheatley had become like the soothsayer, for the strangest knowledge of a prophet is that what must be will be, no matter the purity of intention or strength of will of those who would seek to change their fate. The greater the prophet, the more certainly does he or she accept this truth as it applies to his or her own life. While no material benefit came to Wheatley as a result of her meeting with Washington, a greater significance permeated this meeting of a slave girl with the most powerful man in the colonies. Antony fell upon his sword in grief at the news that Cleopatra had died, news that Cleopatra herself had sent to him because she feared his wrath at the refusal of her Egyptian army to aid him at the battle of Alexandria. Antony, on the verge of death, was brought to Cleopatra and breathed his last in her arms before she could articulate what lay closest to her heart. Wheatley's poem is both a panegyric and a warning, but it holds something more. It is also infused with love—not the passion of first love, but rather the selflessness of last love. Phillis Wheatley willingly sacrificed herself in order to inspire the Idea of the Good to manifest in her beloved.

The life of Phillis Wheatley was a tragedy. The signal events in the second half of her life recall the terrifying deeds of Medea, as portrayed in the play of Euripides, in a manner that suggests divine justice, in its even-handed way, had transformed Medea's vengeance into the destiny that came to descend on Wheatley's head. Phillis married a man named Peters, who later abandoned her and took her second, and probably most significant, book of poetry with him when he left. This second book, which may have proven to her fellow citizens that a former slave was truly capable of composing such pure poetry, was lost forever. She experienced utter poverty and died of exposure in a bitter, New England winter along with her two children, one of whom was found wrapped in her arms. That a poet should have to lead such a life is the stuff of tragedy, but little novelty. That the Poet of the Revolution, the Namer of Columbia, and the herald of Washington's glory is still unrecognized shows how truly selfless Phillis Wheatley had become—how like her beloved in wishing all for him and nothing for herself.

chapter three

THE REVOLUTIONARY WAR

The Revolutionary War began in the town that later served as the birthplace of American culture. The Battle of Concord marked the beginning of armed combat in the War for Independence from Great Britain, and historians generally relate it to other engagements in the vicinity of Boston, grouping them together and characterizing the whole as the first stage of war. The strategy of the British army occupying Boston was to find and crush the insurgent rebels. This strictly attacking strategy was foiled for a second time some two months after Paul Revere's ride when General Howe attacked the colonial militia at Breed's Hill and suffered withering casualties before finally forcing the colonials from the field. The capture of Fort Ticonderoga by Ethan Allen and Benedict Arnold, and the subsequent transfer of its cannons by Henry Knox to the high ground around Boston, made the British strategy unworkable. General Howe evacuated his troops to sea in March of 1776, lifting the siege of Boston. The signing of the Declaration of Independence three months later was the formal cause of the war and ended the war's first stage.

The first stage of the War for Independence included a military operation of General Washington that is less well known than the shot heard round the world or the declaration of the reasons for separation from Great Britain, largely because the invasion of Canada proved to be so ineffective. The attempt to involve the "fourteenth colony" in the rebellion experienced early success with the capture of Montreal by a force under the command of Brigadier General Montgomery. Even as Montgomery made his progress towards Montreal, Washington gave the brave, young Benedict Arnold a commission in the army and ordered him north with a second force to capture the city of Quebec. In a month-long portage and march down raging rivers, through bog-laden forests, and over towering mountains, Arnold lost almost half his men, and the remainder were starved and ragged when they stumbled out onto the plains before the city at the opening of the cold Canadian winter. Quebec's inaccessible location and stout defenders stymied the creative tactics of Benedict Arnold, who braved "the hot gates" but was carried from the field with a bullet in his leg. Nineteen-year-old Aaron Burr ascended icy cliffs in Montgomery's parallel attack on Quebec, but was repelled by Canadian gunnery. The youthful American leaders withdrew from the Battle of Quebec with an army that lacked its general, for Montgomery himself was one of the casualties. The remainder of the army, under Burr's undaunted leadership, took up siege positions around the city, but despite periodic reinforcements could gain no advantage over the garrison within. Finally conceding defeat with the arrival of an overwhelming contingent of British regulars under General Burgoyne, Burr retreated south and arrived back on American soil just as the Declaration of Independence was being signed. The actions of the two most controversial of the Founding Fathers gave promise of their daring and courage.

  The second stage of the Revolutionary War began with the Battle of Long Island in August, 1776. General Howe and the admiral of the British fleet, his brother, sought out the Continental Army, while General Washington fortified the high ground in Brooklyn. The Redcoats won the battle by flanking the patriot forces and capturing or killing over two thousand soldiers. General Washington evacuated Long Island with the help of the artillery company stationed at Harlem Heights, led by the youthful Alexander Hamilton. General Howe pursued the Continental Army and won minor battles at White Plains and Fort Washington, but his overly cautious conduct of the war spared the Continentals to fight another day as he waited for reinforcements and failed to attack when Washington's forces were still within striking distance. After the Continental Army's retreat to Newark, General Howe seemed always one step behind as he chased his foe across the Jerseys to Trenton, where the Delaware River halted his army for the winter. Some historians point to the fog covering the evacuation of Long island and other fortuitous events as Providence assisting Washington and turning the delays of General Howe into major blunders. The miraculous escapes of Washington during the French and Indian War were but a prelude to his preservation of the Continental Army during its four-month-long retreat from Long Island.

  The Continental Army numbered less than four thousand men when it arrived on the west bank of the Delaware River. With this exhausted and poorly-equipped force, Washington chose to engage a fully-outfitted, professional army twice its size. He launched his campaign with a surprise attack against the Hessian garrison at Trenton on Christmas Eve of 1776. Hamilton's artillery played a key role in subduing and capturing over nine hundred of the German mercenaries—along with their cannons, munitions, supplies, colors, and even band instruments—with the loss of only one private and a single officer. Washington next stumped the generalship of Cornwallis and moved the Continental Army to Princeton, New Jersey. After a stunning victory there, he at last met the brilliant, young Hamilton and soon made him his personal aide. The audacity of Washington's counter-attack, the brilliance of his tactics, and the firmness of his leadership led future military historians to include the Ten-Day Campaign in their courses. It filled the American people with hope and impressed foreign observers as well. When the army of Count Rochambeau finally arrived in America, the French king placed it under Washington's command.

After withdrawing his army to New York City for the winter months, General Howe left Long Island in July, 1777, to resume the attack and capture the lone jewel in Columbia's crown, Philadelphia. British strategy had changed while he wintered in New York, but General Howe was not informed about it until he had already set sail for the Delaware River. The situation on the ground called for a more positional strategy instead of the attack-and-pursuit of the previous year. General Howe was ordered to sail up the Hudson River to meet a second force coming down from Canada—General Burgoyne's army, which had driven Benedict Arnold out of Canada a year earlier—at the midway point, Albany. The idea of separating New England from the other colonies, of dividing and conquering, was sound strategy; fortunately for the fledgling republic, it was not successfully implemented. Instead, General Howe continued to seek out the Continental Army, which had wintered in Morristown, and bested Washington at the Battle of Brandywine in September. Aaron Burr provided one of the few bright spots for the American side that September, just days after the defeat at the Brandywine River. Granted the command of Colonel Malcolm's regiment near Suffern in New Jersey, Burr moved south and routed a British picket at Hackensack, though Burr's refusal to obey his commander's order to delay the attack landed him in trouble. Later that month, General Howe sent the Continental Congress fleeing as he entered Philadelphia and garrisoned British troops in Carpenter's Hall, just above the room where the Declaration of Independence was signed. He was confident that he had struck a decisive blow against the rebellion.

The turning point of the Revolutionary War occurred scarce weeks after the demoralizing fall of Philadelphia. General Burgoyne, in his bid to divide the colonies, had led the British army stationed in Canada down Lake Champlain and taken Fort Ticonderoga in August. The British advance seemed set to surge forward through upstate New York, but from that point on the British march slowed as the retreating rebel forces moved along in front, felling huge trees across the roads and forcing the invading army literally to cut its way through the woods along the Hudson River. In the midst of the agonizing twenty-three day march that covered only twenty-one miles, the morning watch found a letter nailed to a tree warning General Burgoyne, "Thus far shalt thou go and no further." Burgoyne's obstacles only multiplied when the eyes of the army, his four hundred Iroquois scouts, melted away and American frontiersmen took bead on John Bull's blinded Redcoats. The American army, under General Gates, easily dispatched Burgoyne's desperate attempts to send for help. The series of engagements that sealed the fate of the world's greatest fighting force and tipped the scales of divine justice to Columbia's side took place in the vicinity of Saratoga. The honor of the victory belonged to Benedict Arnold, whose leadership matched his heroism in the ensuing Battle of Bemis Heights. As if taunting the British commander after his own Canadian misadventure in the wilderness, Arnold himself had tacked the letter to Burgoyne to a tree in the general's own camp. Now he personally led his troops against Burgoyne's and drove them into full retreat. Within days the Americans had completely surrounded the demoralized, hungry column of six thousand men. In October of 1777, Burgoyne surrendered.

The rout of Burgoyne's army inspired the patriot cause when it most needed hope, but left open the question of whether General Washington could defeat Howe on the field of battle. The Continental Army faced its great trial at its winter quarters in Valley Forge, Pennsylvania. Washington's men especially needed military training and better discipline. The army was not made up of enlisted men, but of militia whose tour of duty was a single year. Washington himself described their plight and their virtues: "To see Men without Clothes to cover their nakedness, without Blankets to lay on, without Shoes, by which their Marches might be traced by the Blood from their feet is a mark of Patience and obedience which in my opinion can scarce be paralleled." If the Continental Congress did not provide money and provisions and the states failed to send more soldiers, the possibility of defeating the standing army of Britain would seem to be nil. Strangled by a lack of money and fresh troops, sadly lacking in even nominal support from the Congress, Washington's army began a fundamental transformation. While the British troops rested in Philadelphia, American militiamen deserted and returned to their farms. Only indentured servants, former slaves, landless sons, and recent immigrants without prospects of anything better signed on for the duration. Washington took on the task of molding these men into a fighting force with the assistance of the German military expert, Baron von Steuben. Washington's determination to carry out this task, one that seemed impossible to achieve, resembled his willingness to defend Virginia as colonel during the French and Indian War. The act resonated with his legendary perseverance. Yet even the General's personal character was not sufficient to hold together an entire army on the brink of collapse. Thomas Paine arrived in Valley Forge to inspire the troops, and each day at dawn he read to the assembled soldiers those speeches later published as *The Crisis*. Washington himself was in need of inspiration, for his soldiers continued to leave in droves as the general refused to take punitive action to stop the daily desertions. The winter dragged on, endless and bitter, destitute of hope. In February of 1778, Arnold's victory at Saratoga finally bore fruit. The French entered the war and agreed to send troops and a fleet of ships to aid the American cause.

Washington seized the chance to oppose the British army on the field of combat in June, 1778, when the Redcoats, now led by General Clinton, left Philadelphia to return to New York. The Continental Army's training was put to the test at the Battle of Monmouth. Hamilton led the center and Charles Lee one wing, while Burr supported the other. Washington himself had to intervene and rally the troops when Lee failed to execute his orders properly. It has been said of Washington that he believed that he could not be killed. The species of his bravery would be called foolhardiness in any other mortal. The dangers that he faced in the Revolutionary War—and they were many—generally involved Washington entering the scene of battle. At Princeton and again at Monmouth, he joined the battle to rally his troops, but to his mind the risk of death that he incurred was balanced by the necessity of preventing defeat. Washington viewed his personal fate as bound up with the destiny of the Continental Army, and he did not experience fear in what his own troops and officers regarded as the reckless endangerment of the life of their Commander-in-Chief. The kind of scene that could and did scare Washington had occurred at the end of his tenure as leader of the Virginia militia when his forces joined the Forbes campaign and traveled to Fort Duquesne in 1758. On his fourth journey to this region, his regiment encountered a French reconnaissance patrol and began firing. Unfortunately, two groups of his own troops were firing at each other. Washington felt compelled to walk out between them, place his sword on their muskets, and order them to cease firing.

Burr also personally joined the battle at Monmouth in order to save the troops that he had sent into the fray against orders. Washington and Burr's heroism averted a complete debacle, but disobedience, resulting in a court-martial for Lee and disgrace for Burr, prevented Washington from gaining a victory such as he had won in the Battle of Trenton. From a military point of view, the Battle of Monmouth serves as the endpoint of the second stage of the Revolutionary War. In the third stage the focus of the action shifts away from Washington to battles fought elsewhere: in the West with William Rogers Clark, at sea with John Paul Jones, and in the South with Nathanael Greene. The beginning of this third stage is signaled by a significant change in British strategy as large numbers of troops move to seaports in the South.

A more literary point of view augments the strictly military viewpoint and helps to clarify the progress of the war, as well as the interrelationship of its events. The first stage of the War for Independence from the viewpoint of the archetypal plot can be called the introduction. Like the initial stage characterized by the military historian, it begins with the call to arms of the Minutemen and lasts until the Declaration of Independence. The second stage, constituting the rising action, begins with the Battle of Long Island and concludes with the capture of Philadelphia and the Pennsylvania State House (later Independence Hall). The third stage of Columbia's story, as it might be called, is the climax, that event which stands by itself and foreshadows the war's outcome with the defeat of the British positional strategy at Saratoga. The next stage encompasses the falling action, its events reflecting those of the rising action in ironic contrast. This fourth stage begins with the entrance of the French army into the war as the counterpart of the occupation of the City of Brotherly love by the British army and continues with the fiasco at Monmouth as the counterpart of the Washington's crossing of the Delaware River. The capture of Savannah in 1778 and Charleston in 1780 are a continuation of the fourth stage and a reflection of the near annihilation of Washington's army on Long Island, the difference being that in 1778 the Union Jack is now flying away from Washington and his men, rather than following them in hot pursuit. The falling action culminates in a turning point that leads to the conclusion, an event that acts as a counterpoint to the Founding Fathers' pledge of their lives, fortunes, and sacred honor. Benedict Arnold, disaffected and angry that his heroism had received such scant reward, sought to deliver to the British what they had failed to gain at Saratoga—access to the Hudson River and military division of the colonies. Hamilton's alertness prevented the surrender of West Point, and Arnold fled on a British warship. Washington was so enraged that he did what no deserter could provoke him to: the court-martial and execution of a soldier, Major André, who had been carrying the letters that exposed the treasonous plot.

In October, 1780, a month after Arnold's treason, the fifth stage of the Revolutionary War began with the Battle of King's Mountain. Historians often compare this battle to Breed's Hill for its bitterness. King's Mountain took on special significance for the patriot cause since only a single British soldier took part in the fray. The battle for King's Mountain was fought by a spontaneously assembled force of patriot irregulars against British-trained Tories, colonials loyal to the Crown and working with the British army to suppress the rebellion. General Nathanael Greene, often considered to be second only to Washington in his military prowess, had been appointed commander of the Southern Department two days before and was not yet in the theater of battle. Cornwallis himself was not nearby and refused to come to the aid of the Tory force. Thus the closing phase of the war opened with American fighting American, the colonials led by John Sevier and Isaac Shelby, the Tories by a British commander, Ferguson. The heroism of Sevier and Shelby won the day, their victory forcing Cornwallis to abandon his campaign in North Carolina and retreat into South Carolina to attempt strategic maneuvers that would force the Americans into open battle. Cornwallis finally accomplished his goal at Guilford Courthouse, drawing the colonial army of Nathanael Greene out into full battle lines across a valley staked out by artillery. Greene lost the field to a British Army that excelled at such set-piece battles, but he was able to effect an orderly retreat and escape with his army intact, while rendering Cornwallis' army incapable of pursuit. The Battle of Guilford Court House drove Cornwallis out of the Carolinas just as Washington's use of the cannons of Ft. Ticonderoga had forced General Howe to evacuate Boston. Outmaneuvered, Cornwallis withdrew to Virginia and joined in the game of chasing Jefferson and Lafayette, excellent horsemen both, around the countryside. While this fox-and-hare diversion made the Virginia governor the subject of much ridicule, the scorn of his critics did not make him begrudge the Continental Army the troops his state had sent. Nor did he lose sight of the opportunity that now presented itself.

    Of the 10,000 letters that Jefferson penned in his lifetime, the ones to Washington and the French admiral in the summer of 1781 were among the most important. General Washington embraced Jefferson's outline of the tactics required to end the war and began a forced march to the Yorktown peninsula, contacting Admiral DeGrasse and pleading with him for the French navy to prevent a British escape by sea. Within a month the Continental Army, along with the 5,000-man French contingent of Count Rochambeau, completed the journey, averaging over twenty miles per day and finally bottling up the British forces on the Virginia coast. The Battle of Yorktown in October, 1781, revealed more of Hamilton's character. His ambition had chafed under his role as aide; he had finally resigned under a pretext in February 1781, but later begged to be given a command of troops. At Yorktown, the General gave his aide the chance to prove his mettle. Washington stood up in his bunker as bullets flew around him and his aides prayed for him to step down. He watched Hamilton lead the American column that captured the first redoubt of the British fortifications at Yorktown. With the strong point of his defenses in Hamilton's hands and a bombardment from the French fleet providing cover, General Cornwallis had little choice but to surrender. He grudgingly accepted defeat and withdrew his army to New York. Within months, England entered into peace negotiations.

With the cessation of hostilities, the Commander-in-chief set about the task of disbanding the Continental Army, which he completed on December 23, 1783 at a special session of Congress in Annapolis. Wheatley's prophecy in 1775 exhorted Washington to hold Columbia first and foremost in his heart. Washington's surrender of his commission to the Congress marked one of the pivotal events in the history of the nation, a moment of selfless action that set the tone and direction for the future of this fragile experiment in government by the people. Congress had been unkind to Washington on many occasions, denying him money and supplies, even going so far as to publicly question his fitness to prosecute the war when events had been at their darkest. Congress had a record of making few friends in the army as well; months before Yorktown, two mutinies had broken out over pay and terms of enlistment, one of which was put down only when Washington dispatched troops to the scene and executed the ringleaders.

The proposition of disbanding a standing army in the field is complex in any circumstances, but in the uncertain and heady months following Yorktown, as the peace negotiations dragged on to uncertain end, it proved to be a task on the order of a Herculean labor. The states were functioning politically and economically as little more than a loose confederation, and Congress was deeply divided about what a peacetime government should look like. Washington himself received letters suggesting the only hope for saving the country from corruption and collapse was the establishment of a monarchy, bolstered by the army—with Washington serving as king. Doubts about the ability of Congress to accomplish even the most basic functions prompted a group of officers to condemn the body and threaten revolt if they did not receive their due compensation. Hamilton, now a member of Congress and chair of the committee charged with disbursing funds and settling the debts of Congress through the States, wrote to Washington about his concern over the rumors of the army's discontent and suggested that Washington himself had not done enough to press the army's case before Congress, and that it was his responsibility to regain control of the military for the sake of domestic tranquility. In point of fact, only Washington's personal force and gravitas could diffuse the situation. He made a bold appearance at a meeting of his officers, striding into the room and roundly condemning the seditious plan as insidious and distasteful in the highest degree. After laying out the reasons for his opposition and guaranteeing his personal commitment to tirelessly seek justice on their behalf from the Congress, Washington exhorted his men,

> Let me conjure you, in the name of our common Country, as you value your own sacred honor, as you respect the rights of humanity, and as you regard the Military and National character of America, to express your utmost horror and detestation of the Man who wishes, under any specious pretences, to overturn the liberties of our Country, and who wickedly attempts to open the flood Gates of Civil discord, and deluge our rising Empire in Blood.†

When Washington left the room, his officers—to a man—foreswore the plot and signaled the allegiance of the army to the civilian government. The meeting, which had taken place at army headquarters in Newburgh, occurred on the Ides of March.

Six months later, just under two years after Cornwallis' surrender at Yorktown, Britain signed a treaty with her colonies, recognizing them as a new and independent nation. Soon thereafter, the British army withdrew from New York. The last of the Redcoats left America soil. In December, Washington bade

---

† "Speech to the Officers of the Army," March 15, 1783. In *George Washington: Writings*. Library of America, 1997. p.500.

farewell to his officers, then made his way to appear before Congress at Annapolis. The great hero of the war, the most powerful man in the nation, not only surrendered his command of the army, but rejected any claim to public office or position of influence whatsoever in the new government. A painting by Edwin Blashfield of the event at Annapolis gave artistic confirmation of the deeper significance of Washington's determination to forego any personal glory or mantle of kingship. Columbia sits on a throne, attended by her consorts and flanked by soldiers of the Revolution. Washington stands to her left, indicating his loyal service to Columbia with a single gesture as he lays his commission at her feet and retires, a private citizen.

Some seven months earlier, not long after the affair at Newburgh, Washington founded a society for his officers and their descendents, the Society of the Cincinnati, ostensibly to honor the patriotism of those who, like the Roman general, Cincinnatus, had left their farms to lead the defense of their country against an invader and were now about to return thence. George Washington was rumored to be a member, even a Grand Master, of a Freemasonic lodge, and this new society apparently took such a lodge as its model and kept to the oath of secrecy. The name of this organization suggests that its secrets have to do with the connection of America to ancient Rome. Washington's relation to Hercules is the open secret of America's founding, though whether this idea originated with the Society of the Cincinnati cannot be determined. Shakespeare's play introduces the further relation of Hercules to Antony, a relationship that Plutarch suggests the Roman people believed in and that Antony encouraged:

> He had also a good and noble appearance; his beard was well grown, his forehead large, and his nose aquiline, giving him altogether a bold, masculine look that reminded people of the faces of Hercules in paintings and sculptures. It was, moreover, an ancient tradition, that the Antonys were descended from Hercules, by a son of his called Anton; and this opinion he thought to give credit to by the similarity of his person just mentioned, and also by the fashion of his dress.†

The personalities of Hercules, Antony, and Washington may well be tied together by spiritual threads like those said to have been woven by the three Fates.

Prior to his relationship with Cleopatra and the civil war with Octavian, Antony was most well known for his involvement in the swirl of events that led to the murder of Julius Caesar in the Senate. When tribune of the people and later in the office of augur, Marc Antony supported Caesar against Pompey. After joining Caesar's army, he became his greatest captain, defeating Pompey at the decisive battle of Pharsalia. Antony was true to Caesar until the very end and even after. One need not look far for a compatriot as close to Washington as Antony was to Caesar before finding a telling clue: Alexander Hamilton often used the pseudonym of Julius Caesar when writing the essays that later became known as *The Federalist Papers*. The relationship between Washington and Hamilton is a curious

---

† *Plutarch's Lives.* Arthur Hugh Clough, trans. Modern Library Classics, volume II.483.

reversal of that between Antony and Caesar, hinting at the debt that Caesar owed Antony for his loyalty and support, and for turning public opinion against the conspirators after his death, so that they were scattered and hunted. Such an insight helps to illuminate Hamilton's character: his undying loyalty to Washington, his innate talent for leadership, his vanity, and his desire to please the wealthy. Antony owed Caesar a debt as well, not one for help that Caesar gave him, but for a deed Antony had failed to accomplish, one that had dire consequences for the people that they governed. On the day of Caesar's murder, the 15th of March, Marc Antony was kept from the Senate by a long conversation contrived for that purpose. He could not prevent the three-and-twenty stab wounds that took Caesar's life. On the same day in 1783, almost at Hamilton's behests, Washington turned aside the knives that his own officers would have plunged into the body politic, sparing the fledgling American republic and safeguarding the government of the people.

chapter four

BENJAMIN FRANKLIN

There is one Founding Father who held an equal place with Washington and shared the highest esteem of his contemporaries: the printer, philosopher, inventor, and diplomat, Benjamin Franklin. As a backdrop to his many pursuits, Franklin was a member of a Freemasonic order, which he joined in 1731 at the age of twenty-five. Historians suspect that almost all of the Founders were Masons—fifty-three of the fifty-six signers of the Declaration were confirmed or suspected members—but Franklin's membership is an historical fact since he published the *Constitutions of the Free-Masons* in 1734. His *Autobiography*, probably the foremost work of American literature in the eighteenth century, included a passage that explained how he (or any other person, as he suggested) was able to accomplish so much. He unveiled the path of virtue, which is the heart and soul of Freemasonry,—the daily exercise of the virtues of temperance, silence and the other moral qualities and how to achieve them. *Poor Richard's Almanac*,—published regularly for twenty-five years,—was in many respects Franklin's attempt to bring this Masonic secret to the common man in the form of epigrams. Yet Franklin was not one to suggest that as weighty an undertaking as the perfection of character could practicably be achieved in a human lifetime, even by exercising a rigorous self-discipline. By way of indication, he wrote his epitaph at the beginning of his career. In it he told, not of his achievements, but of one of the great secrets of Freemasonry, that this life is but a preparation for another and better life when the spirit will incarnate again on earth.

> The body of
> B. Franklin, Printer;
> (Like the cover of an old book,
> Its contents worn out,
> and stripped of its lettering and gilding)
> Lies here, food for worms.
> But the work shall not be lost:
> For it will, (as he believed) appear once more,
> In a new and more elegant edition,
> Revised and corrected
> By the Author.

Franklin's contributions to the social life of his adopted city of Philadelphia began when he organized a debating club called the Junto, which lasted for forty years. Four years later at age twenty-five, he started the first circulating library. By age thirty he had involved his fellow citizens in numerous civic projects that transformed the frontier town into a world-class city. Franklin became the postmaster of Philadelphia,—a position that he held for twenty-one years,—and organized a fire department. The following year he helped usher in Philadelphia's first constables. Franklin also founded an academy, which has since become the University of Pennsylvania. The establishment of a hospital, the paving of streets, and the addition of streetlights completed the transformation. This outer activity of citizens working together for the common good, a process that took thirty years, provides the basis for characterizing Franklin as the Father of American Civilization. General Howe's desire to seize this city and enjoy its comforts is understandable, but if he thought that the citizens who built it out of their own initiative would be cowed by its occupation, he was sadly mistaken. Franklin was hurt both personally and materially by Howe's deed, but his consolation was that his creation helped entice General Howe to make what was most likely the greatest blunder of the Revolutionary War. When asked by the French about the significance of Howe's capture of the city, Franklin replied, "it was not he who had taken Philadelphia, but instead Philadelphia who had taken him."

Franklin's concern for civic affairs extended beyond the confines of Philadelphia to the political relationships among the colonies and the form of government most suitable for them. A conference held in Albany, New York, in 1745, in which the sachem of the Iroquois Confederation were to present their idea of proper governance, piqued his interest. One whole volume of his collected works is devoted to Franklin's notes on the speeches of the tribal leaders of the Six Nations. The six principles of government that the sachem discussed had spread beyond the borders of the Iroquois League even before the arrival of the Puritans at Plymouth Rock, as the six principles contained in the peace treaty that the Pilgrims signed with Massasoit attests. Franklin worked over these ideals of government in the following years until General Braddock's army arrived in America and forced the issue of what model the colonies might adopt in order to govern their own interests. Like Washington,

Franklin observed British incompetence first hand as he took on the thankless task of provisioning Braddock's troops, often at his own expense. What he had written about in 1747 in a pamphlet entitled *Plain Truth*,—that the British army was incapable of providing for the defense of the American colonies,—led, in 1754, to his call for a confederation of states and the publication of the Albany Plan as a practical way to achieve it. The French and Indian War began in the same year, and the Native American tribes sided with the French. One exception was the Iroquois League, which had always supported the British and continued to do so even until the time that General Burgoyne began his invasion from Canada on the road to Saratoga. The desertion of Burgoyne's four hundred Iroquois scouts—who refused to assist Burgoyne's army in fighting the Americans—was an important factor in the victory at Saratoga, the turning point of the Revolutionary War.

In 1757 Ben Franklin traveled to England to represent the concerns of Pennsylvania over the colonial policies of Great Britain. For the next eighteen years he was the spokesman for colonial interests, gradually agreeing to the requests of other colonies for him to be their representative. On his voyages back and forth over the Atlantic Ocean he discovered the Gulf Stream by dropping a thermometer in the water and recording the differences in temperature. The difficulties of his job increased with the passage of the Stamp Act and the protests that it engendered. His skill as a mediator and his superb sense of humor helped the colonies gain friends in Parliament as well as among the English people, some of whom, like Thomas Paine, made their way to America at his invitation. His activities included participation in cultural events, and during his stay in London he even invented a new musical instrument. His Masonic activities also continued there, though not as publicly and without the fanfare they would later receive in France. While Franklin's actual influence in London is difficult to quantify, the opposition of Britain's own people to the war would prove to be a significant factor in the eventual American victory.

There is a great deal of Freemasonic literature supporting the idea that Masons helped to found the United States of America. While much of it is self-serving and lacks historical documentation, it is at least worthwhile to consider the Masonic viewpoint given Franklin's public acknowledgement of his Masonic ties. There are few satisfactory scenarios that explain how a disparate group of farmers, townsmen, and merchants managed to pull off the logistical, political, economic, and military coordination necessary to oppose the Redcoats in concert, particularly given the volatile disagreement that so often threatened a ruinous end to the entire enterprise. Viewing the Sons of Liberty as members of lodges sets a logical context for their communication, organization, and dedication, making Paul Revere's ride, the stockpiles of munitions, and the heroic Battle of Concord more understandable. Masonic authors reason that these lodges were able to oppose the mightiest army in the world because the Mother Lodge in England had already granted them their autonomy and they deemed political independence certain to follow. The Grand Master of the American lodges was said to be James Warren, who helped to defend Breed's Hill and became one of the casualties. John Hancock was said to be the leader of the Boston lodge; as President of the Second Continental Congress, he became the first to sign his name to the document declaring America's political independence. Hancock was also widely supposed to have been the organizer behind the Boston Tea Party. Why he had the Sons of Liberty dress in Native American costume may have a deeper significance than historians generally allow. Franklin's insight into the importance of the Iroquois traditions was probably not lost on those fellow Masons who had read the Albany Plan and later adopted the Articles of Confederation. The Sons of Liberty took their name not from an abstract ideal, but from a spirit that was native to this land. Early depictions of Columbia in her guise as Liberty showed her as an Indian Princess. Though the idea that Columbia was directly associated with the native peoples of North America was abroad in popular culture, it was Walt Whitman, in the middle of the next century, who would the bring connection of the spirit of Liberty with the homeland of the Iroquois Confederation,—in the area of the Great Lakes and southward,—into the public consciousness.

> By Blue Ontario's shore,
> As I mused of these warlike days and of peace return'd
>   and the dead that return no more,
> A Phantom gigantic superb, with stern visage accosted me,
> *Chant me the poem,* it said, *that comes from the soul of*
>   *America, chant me the carol of victory,*
> *And strike up the marches of Libertad, marches more*
>   *powerful yet,*
> *And sing me before you go the song of the throes of*
>   *Democracy.*†

---

† "By Blue Ontario's Shore." In *Leaves of Grass.* Library of America, Vintage Books, 1992. p.468.

A deeper study of the influence of Freemasonry on the American Revolution would be possible if more public figures, in addition to Ben Franklin, had professed their membership. There is, however, a most significant leader of the Freemasonic movement who became something like a counterpart of Franklin. Just as there is a rule in the Masonic lodges that a public figure should not reveal his ties to a lodge, that it remain secret, so too is there a rule that a high initiate should not become a public figure, but should remain in the background. Franklin broke the former rule; the Count of St. Germain the latter. While he is still a shadowy figure, certain historical facts are known about the Count of St. Germain, one of which is that he was in England in 1760 at the same time as Franklin. He is also known to have conducted experiments with Mesmer in Germany in 1766 and to have met with Marie Antoinette in 1770. His importance for Freemasons is bound up with the belief that he was the reincarnation of Christian Rosenkreutz and that he was also the original founder of the order of Freemasonry. That the French Masons selected the Count of St. Germain as their chief representative for a conference in 1785 is in line with this belief. The mission of such a man is shrouded to some degree in mystery, and its high purpose involves what is called esoterically the Temple Legend, a Masonic story told of Hiram's work as the first builder and architect of the Temple of Solomon, the sacred dwelling place of the Ark of the Covenant. The Freemasons were called Masons because, as their traditions maintain, their earliest members had erected monumental buildings such as the great cathedrals of Europe. The building that St. Germain wanted to build was not a physical temple, but one formed out of the sincere strivings of men and women after the highest ideals. A comparison with Franklin illuminates this central teaching of the Masonic lodges. Though Franklin did little of the physical labor required to transform Philadelphia into the City of Brotherly Love, his vision and ability to inspire virtue in others stand behind it. Franklin, the lone exoteric leader to acknowledge his connection with Freemasonry, was able to bring its inspiring force to the common man and construct social institutions based on civic virtues. The Count of St. Germain, the lone esoteric leader to appear as a public figure, wished to inspire the Freemasons themselves that they might shape something in the realm of thought. He wished to create a spiritual temple based on the theological virtues of faith, hope, and love.

Modern Freemasonic literature emphasizes the importance of the relation of Franklin and St. Germain to Masonic traditions, though again the historic facts are difficult to verify. Manly P. Hall, a Freemasonic author, gives certain instances of the Count of St. Germain working together with Benjamin Franklin. The most important collaboration involved their work with Thomas Jefferson on the Declaration of Independence. This document represents the kind of thought-construct that the Count of St. Germain hoped to achieve, and its central theme is the thought that he wished to introduce to the world—that all men are created equal. The story goes that Jefferson became more and more depressed as the delegates to the Second Continental Congress deleted and changed more and more of his draft, while Franklin sat next to him and comforted him. With the task of revision completed, indecision and anxiety swept over the participants. A stranger (said to be St. Germain) appeared in the room and began to speak, and enthusiasm burned anew in the audience. Franklin then spoke his famous words: "Gentlemen, we must all hang together or, most assuredly, we shall all hang separately;" and the delegates arose en masse and hurried up to Hancock's desk to emulate his example. Another instance concerns the American flag. Manly Hall credits Franklin for coming up with a design and the Count of St. Germain for offering an alternative. Jefferson had the task of comforting Franklin and telling him that the design of the Count of St. Germain was the better one. The perfection of the American flag,—distinguished by its balance of colors, which were originally described as white for purity and innocence, red for hardiness and valor, and blue for vigilance, perseverance, and justice,—has an effect on the American people that is unparalleled to this day. For many Americans the idea of desecrating the flag in any way is tantamount to burning the Christian Bible.

During the war years Franklin served his country as ambassador to France. He gradually became the symbol of America for the French people, moving easily among the social circles of the French nobility while sporting his coonskin cap. It was he who garnered French support for America after the Battle of Saratoga, and he again who—working with John Adams—negotiated the Treaty of Paris that ended the conflict in 1783. Thus did Franklin replicate in Paris the successes that he had achieved earlier in Philadelphia and in London. His Masonic activities in France were well known, and he was even given the title of Venerable or Grand Master at the Court of the Nine Sisters, the leading Freemasonic lodge in Paris. It was in this capacity that he may have become privy to a significant insight into the mystery of Columbia. The nine Sisters, or the nine Muses, were daughters of Apollo and Mnemosyne and were said to serve Apollo by inspiring the masterful artistic creations of ancient Greece. One Muse in particular, the goddess of epic poetry called Calliope, had the task of founding the culture of ancient Greece: "O Muse, speak through me the wrath of Achilles." Just as Walt Whitman had unveiled the connection of the spirit of America to the homeland of the Iroquois Confederation, so did he illustrate the relation of America's nation spirit to Calliope. In 1871, he published "Song of the Exposition" and traced out Calliope's continued activity down through the ages in Rome and in the various emerging European countries until the appearance of her greatest masterpiece, Dante's *Divine Comedy*. Whitman, who wrote perhaps more poems to or about Columbia than any other poet, then pointed to her presence in the Exposition itself—how the Greek goddess envisioned by Phillis Wheatley was visible to him amid the new inventions on display:

> I say I see, my friends, if you do not, the illustrious
>   émigré,(having it is true in her day, although the same,
>   changed, journey'd considerable,)
> Making directly for this rendezvous, vigorously clearing a
>   path for herself, striding through the confusion,
> By thud of machinery and shrill steam-whistle undismay'd,
> Bluff'd not a bit by drain-pipe, gasometers, artificial
>   fertilizers,
> Smiling and pleas'd with palpable intent to stay,
> She's here, install'd amid the kitchen ware!
>
> But hold—don't I forget my manners?

To introduce the stranger, (what else indeed do I live to
   chant for?) to thee Columbia;
In liberty's name welcome immortal! Clasp hands,
And ever henceforth sisters dear be both.†

Any characterization of Ben Franklin would be incomplete without mention of his inventions and scientific treatises, especially the one presenting his theory of electricity. During his stay in London, he was invited to become a member of the prestigious Royal Society. In Paris he was active in the French Academy of the Sciences, which had many members also known to participate in the Court of the Nine Muses. The Count of St. Germain was reported to have appeared in Paris twice during Franklin's stay there. When Mesmer, the protégé of St. Germain, arrived in Paris in 1784, the French Academy offered to study the phenomenon of "animal magnetism," also called mesmerism or hypnotism, and write up a formal report. Choosing a member of the Academy for this task proved difficult, and the French king had to settle the dispute. The French scientists were taken aback when one of their number was not selected. The king chose an American, Ben Franklin, to observe and issue a scientific finding on its meaning.

The period of Franklin's life toward the end of his stay in Paris earned a descriptive name in the popular consciousness, one that recalls Wheatley's prophecy for Washington as well as Brumidi's masterpiece. His achievements there became known as Franklin's apotheosis. Artists of the time also recognized that

---

† "Song of the Exposition." In *Leaves of Grass*. Library of America, Vintage Books, 1992. p.468.

the deeds of Franklin had such a spiritual import, that his actions had prepared him for a kind of "deification" at the time of his passing over the threshold of death. "The Apotheosis of Washington and Franklin," a print on a cotton textile in 1790, was widely disseminated in commemoration of Franklin's death. The print showed Washington driving a chariot pulled by leopards as Columbia rode in the car behind him. Franklin walked ahead, leading the way towards Columbia's home. The two foremost of the Founding Fathers, having achieved the high purpose of the path of virtue that both had followed, continued their service to Columbia in her temple, the Temple of Liberty.

The earliest artistic representations of Columbia tended to separate the two aspects of Indian Princess (harking back to her activity as the Native American spirit, Iroquoia) and of Greek Goddess (relating to her mission as Muse). Henry Gardiner, in a print from 1784 entitled "Governors of Ye United States of America," called the former, "America," and the latter, "Independence." As America sat and looked on, Franklin attended her in the garb of a Roman Senator; Washington walked towards the two, hand in hand with Independence. American artists who painted Columbia repeatedly presented her in her two-fold nature as the goddess of Peace and Brotherhood, with the olive branch and shield, and as the warlike goddess of Liberty, with the red cap and sword, often in the same picture. A painting from the time of the Civil War, the cover of sheet music for a song entitled "Honor to Washington," showed an artist's view of Columbia's dual aspect and her champion, George Washington.

The eagle, the symbol that the Founding Fathers found

"Honor to Washington. A National Ode" (Lithograph, J.H. Bufford, 1859)

appropriate for America and also the emblem of ancient Rome, appeared most often in paintings of Columbia in her aspect as Liberty, protectress of the Republic and defender against tyranny and discord. Liberty, often clad in Athena's armor in these early depictions, seemed to draw her lineage from the Greek Goddess. Yet the Indian Princess had not been forgotten. Though Liberty's attendant, the eagle, won out for depiction on official seals and sigils, it is worth considering that Franklin argued for the turkey to be the national bird. Washington, by declaring the first national day of Thanksgiving, and Lincoln, by making Thanksgiving a perpetual national holiday, led the way for the turkey to receive the recognition that Franklin had envisioned. The turkey, that native American bird, plays the central role in a celebration meant to unite immigrants to this country with those who were native to this land. Thanksgiving is a festival for the extended family. It presents Americans the opportunity to show appreciation for the prosperity and bounty of Columbia in her aspect as goddess of Peace and Brotherhood.

chapter five

THE CONSTITUTION OF THE UNITED STATES OF AMERICA

The Treaty of Paris recognized the United States of America as an independent nation and fulfilled the promise of the Declaration of Independence, but peacetime brought new challenges to the fledgling country. The Articles of Confederation provided little assistance in dealing with difficulties that arose in the areas of business and commerce. Washington retired to Mt. Vernon as a private citizen, but practical problems such as the lack of good roads and trained craftsmen plagued him. When Hamilton took the lead and arranged a conference in Annapolis to try to address the issue of interstate commerce regulation, Washington joined him and gave the conference immense prestige by serving as its president. The participants soon realized that what had been useful during the war years,—a loose confederation of states,—could not meet the challenges of peace. A call went out from the Annapolis Conference for all the states to come together in Philadelphia and work on changing the Articles of Confederation. The following year, in 1787, thirty-three years after Franklin's original call for unity, the Founding Fathers met to give the ideal of the Albany Plan its final form.

The meeting in Philadelphia became a Constitutional

Convention, for no revision could hope to include the myriad of ideas that emerged from the delegates. Although he remained in the background, Franklin's presence at the convention is perhaps the best explanation for the happy outcome of the proceedings. The fortuitous transformations that had occurred in Philadelphia, London, and Paris, were outdone by the creation of one of the great political documents in history. His signature on the Constitution, along with those on the Declaration of Independence and the Articles of Confederation, distinguishes Franklin as the only participant to have signed all three of America's founding works. Washington attended, and the delegates unanimously elected him as president of the Constitutional Convention. Though he presided over all of the meetings, his leadership was of a peculiar type. He only once rose to speak on any of the issues facing the delegates, and that on the very last day of the Convention, yet the representatives in the room with him clearly experienced the powerful influence of his presence. Neither of America's two greatest leaders, however, is credited with the deed itself, but rather the note-taker, James Madison. It is he who is called the Father of the Constitution. Madison had drafted an outline of his vision for a strong central government in a letter to Washington before the Philadelphia convention was set to begin. Over the next few weeks he assembled the ideas he had worked out over the course of a decade, shaped them into clear thoughts, and wove them into a framework, creating a document that rightly belongs with the masterworks of world literature and has served the American people as the longest-lasting constitution of the modern age. The Preamble to the final draft of the Constitution provided a clear statement of the principles that infused the document as a whole. The six stated purposes in the Preamble recall the six principles of the Iroquois League.

The first principle of government listed in the Preamble speaks directly to the difficulties discovered by the states in trying to function as a loose confederation of independent civic entities. Federalism, or the balance of central and distributed power, has become the subject of much debate throughout the nation's history. The ideal of this principle is expressed by the words, "to form a more perfect union," and is included in the name chosen for this country, the United States of America. Hamilton is the Founding Father most closely associated with the principle of federalism, or the means of achieving political union, as indicated by his efforts to increase the powers of the federal government and by the name that he chose both for his book of his essays on the Constitution and for the political party that he founded. In the Constitutional debates, Hamilton seemed to reach almost too far in his conception of federalism, even to miss the idea of balance entirely. In a long speech to the assembled delegates, he argued for a model based on the British system of government and stressed the importance of an "Executive Magistrate" appointed for life. The irony of Hamilton's defense of monarchy was not lost on his audience, many of whom had risked their lives for the ideals of the Declaration of Independence. To a certain extent Alexander Hamilton seemed still to yearn for that which Brutus had denied Caesar: absolute authority invested in a central executive, ratified by the people.

The principle of Union, or federalism, is also called the division of powers. Certain powers,—especially in the areas of commerce, finance, and the military,—are delegated to the federal government, while others,—especially in the areas of education and marriage,—are reserved for the states. Some powers,—such as those concerned with the building of roads, taxation, and the establishment of courts,—are concurrent and belong to both the state and federal governments. This division of powers is incomplete, however, without a third group of powers, the residual powers in the tenth amendment. The Constitution, while establishing the strong central government that Hamilton desired, also includes the Bill of Rights, which was demanded by the states as a condition for abdicating some of their own authority to the central government by ratifying the document. Thus the Constitution ends where it began. "We, the People" are the source of all the enumerated powers, and powers not expressly delegated are reserved for the people. A proper interpretation of the first principle of the preamble, the "more perfect union," depends on the idea that Jefferson stated as a self-evident truth: that these powers belong to the essential nature of the common man, that they are on loan to the representatives of the people. The abuses of such powers make it the people's right, their duty, to throw off such government.

The second principle stated in the Preamble is to "establish justice." The Constitution attempts to infuse the idea of justice into the federal government through a system of checks and balances. The checks on the different branches of government include the Presidential power of veto, the legislative power of impeachment, and the judicial right of review. The balances involve the Presidential power to appoint judges, the bicameral form of Congress and its power to declare war, and the life tenure of Supreme Court justices. Franklin's imprint on the Constitutional Convention appears most clearly in this further development of the basic idea of the Articles of Confederation. Unfortunately, the idea of checks and balances is also called the "separation of powers," which makes it easy to confuse with the principle of the division of powers. Like the division of powers, the separation of powers should be traced back to its source, which is to be found in the people. The separation of the powers of the federal government into three branches implies the consent of the people. Term limits, which are clearly defined for each of the people's representatives (excluding Supreme Court justices to protect their impartiality), lead to elections, which are the means of providing a voice for the people that their will might be heard. Voting is the real check on government.

The third principle of government listed in the Preamble is to "insure domestic tranquility." The abuses of King George III disrupted the peace that the American colonies wished to enjoy, and a clear statement of the rights of man,—a Bill of Rights,—was necessary to forestall tyranny's return in the future. The first amendment to the Constitution guarantees the five freedoms of speech, religion, the press, assembly, and petition. The following nine amendments protect the legal rights of American citizens. The inclusion of the Bill of Rights in the Constitution was the price paid by the Federalists to win Jefferson's support for ratification. Though the ambassador to France was not present during the deliberations of the Constitutional Convention, letters to his protégé, James Madison, ensured that his ideas would become the hallmark of the final document. Jefferson's effort to attain the Neoclassic ideal of transmuting theological articles of faith into the self-evident truths of reason,—embodied in the idea that all men are created equal,—points to a deeper meaning of his contribution to the Constitution. The ten amendments call to mind the deed of Moses and the Ten Commandments, which warned man of the "Thou Shalt" in his relationship to God and the "Thou Shalt Not" in his relationship to his fellow man. From the viewpoint of Neoclassicism and Freemasonry, human beings had made progress in internalizing these prohibitions over the course of three millennia. In the context of the modern ethical consciousness, Jefferson provided a warning, not for man, but for government. Government must protect the liberty of its citizens and not infringe on their enumerated rights.

The next three principles in the Preamble relate to the three branches of government. To "provide for the common defense" is primarily the purpose of the executive branch, whose leader is both President and Commander-in-chief. The purpose to "promote the general welfare" belongs especially to the legislative branch, whose members make laws that should advance this ideal. The purpose to "secure the blessings of liberty" falls to the judicial branch, which should uphold this ideal as it is expressed in the Supreme Law of the land. It was Madison who embedded the concept of a three-folded government in the original draft of the Virginia Plan, the document presented at the opening of the Philadelphia convention that became the template for the Constitution. Madison came to the conclusion that a three-fold government was the strongest and most sustainable model based on years of observing the inefficiencies and weaknesses of the Confederation Congress, observations that led him to review historical and contemporary confederations in search of a better solution in keeping with the spirit of the Revolution. John Adams had reached a similar conclusion as early as 1776, when he wrote a letter entitled "Thoughts on Government" that recommended a three-fold plan of government to the North Carolina assembly, a recommendation that several other states adopted as they established their legislatures. In 1779, upon his return from his first trip to Paris, Adams was invited to draft a constitution for the state of Massachusetts. That document, still the constitution of the Commonwealth today, established a strong executive working with two houses of the legislature and an independent judiciary. Adams returned to this idea with renewed vigor in 1786 and began a monumental survey of every form of Western government from ancient times to the Middle Ages and Renaissance. He reached the conclusion that the rights and liberties of the people could only be preserved through a three-fold government with a strong executive power. Adams, then in England, could not attend as the draft document was hammered out in debate, but his contribution to the Constitutional process was no less vital. The first volume of his *Defence of the Constitutions of Government of the United States of America* appeared just after the Philadelphia convention released the Constitution to the states for ratification. It became a popular and compelling argument in support of the proposed new government. The idea that man is a three-fold being is as old as Plato, who discussed it two millennia ago in the *Republic*. Whereas Plato applied the concept of three-folding to society as a whole, Adams and Madison brought it into the field of political science. This same idea also appears in Freemasonry as the doctrine of the three pillars of strength, beauty, and wisdom, names that also refer to the virtues of each of the three branches of government in turn—the Executive, the Legislative, and the Judicial. Late in life, Adams recalled that the earliest memory of his childhood was being told of the continual progress of the three pillars of empire, art, and science from East to West. Their journey from Europe over the Atlantic to America completed the Great Circle.

 Despite deep misgivings about the Constitution, Hamilton shouldered the task of winning its passage by the states. Working with Madison on a series of articles that became *The Federalist Papers*, he provided the rationale that persuasively defended the bedrock principles of the Constitution against the well-organized attacks of the Anti-Federalists and established the basis of Constitutional thought to this day. Hamilton personally joined in the heated discussions of the New York State Assembly and attempted to convince recalcitrant members to adopt the Constitution, but the Anti-Federalists were firmly in control of the convention and successfully resisted ratification even as many of the smaller states quickly approved the new Constitution. Meanwhile in Virginia, Madison led the struggle against the deeply entrenched Anti-Federalists of that state in the most crucial contest for ratification, finally defeating Patrick Henry and his allies in debate. Virginia ratified just days after New Hampshire, fulfilling the two-thirds requirement for passage of the Constitution into law. With the establishment of the new government certain, many of New York's Anti-Federalists bowed to Hamilton's position. The largest state in the Confed-

The Constitution

"America, with Peace and Freedom Blest!" (Etching, The Columbian Magazine, 1789)

eration finally ratified by a margin of just three votes.

In his farewell address to Congress in December of 1784, General Lafayette offered a benediction that "this immense temple of freedom Ever Stand a lesson to oppressors, an Example to the oppressed, a Sanctuary for the Rights of Mankind." In 1787, the year the Constitutional Convention drafted the plan for the new government, a congressman from Pennsylvania prophesied that America's federal government would "lay a foundation for erecting Temples of Liberty in every part of the earth." In the

"Behold! a fabric now to freedom rear'd" (Etching, The Columbian Magazine, 1788)

ratification contest, the idea that the people were building the Temple of Liberty—a spiritual edifice, a structure of thought—pervaded the national consciousness. Every state that ratified was deemed to be a pillar of the temple of freedom. On July 4th, 1788, a procession in Philadelphia to honor the ratification featured a float with a domed temple having ten pillars, one for each of the states that had ratified. The "Federal Edifice" built for the parade appeared on the cover of *The Columbian Magazine* as the temple in "America, with Peace and Freedom Blest."

Following the Philadelphia parade, James Trenchard published a print of a classical temple with thirteen columns and an inscription across the lintel, "Sacred to Liberty, Justice, and Peace." These three principles stand atop the Temple in the form of goddesses; in the foreground, Columbia's winged son hands her a parchment of the Constitution and points to the temple, as if to show her the home that the States have built for her. Finally, in 1789, Congress formally ratified the first ten amendments to the Constitution and brought to realization Lafayette's benediction: the Bill of Rights was enshrined in the Temple of Liberty's innermost sanctum.

Hamilton and Madison—the driving force behind the Constitution and its author—joined together to bring about its ratification and, that accomplished, took their positions at opposite ends of the political spectrum. They did unite one last time in what historians call "the deal," the exchange of mutual support for the political project that each one held most dear. Hamilton's fiscal plan for the new government depended on restoring the nation's public credit by centralizing the management of the tangled mass of foreign and domestic debt, including debt belonging to the individual states. The Southern states, led by Madison and the Virginians, vigorously opposed Hamilton's design because they had paid down more of their wartime debt than the Northern states and thought it unfair to have to shoulder an additional burden, in the form of federal taxes, for debt they had not themselves incurred. Jefferson, though himself a Virginian, recognized the essential need for the nation to have good credit abroad and encouraged Madison to accept Hamilton's proposal to allow the federal government to assume the states' wartime debt in return for Hamilton's support for a site for the nation's capital that was closer to the Southern states—indeed, on Virginia's border. After a dinner party at Jefferson's residence in June, 1790, Hamilton and Madison withdrew to a private sitting room and made the deal. The larger importance of centralizing the nation's debt for Hamilton soon became clear. The following year he achieved his overriding purpose, the establishment of a national bank. Less clear is why Jefferson placed such value on what was originally called "Washington, in the Territory of Columbia."

One of the mysteries of Jefferson's life is how he found time to do so much. His interest in the project of laying out the capital competed for the next six years with his responsibilities as Secretary of State and his more famous accomplishment of organizing the Democratic Party. The task of planning the new city was no mean endeavor; it would be the world's only seat of government designed from the ground up, carved out of a hundred square miles of wooded wilderness where no commerce, no institutions, not even any public buildings existed. Jefferson suggested that the planning of the new city be submitted wholly to the discretion and oversight of the chief executive, President Washington, removing the process from legislative debate and the danger that Congress would bottle up the plans in committee. With the adoption of his proposal, Jefferson immediately focused on the design of the city and its principal buildings, becoming Washington's chief consultant on the project. He reviewed the layout of the capital's primary streets and buildings, as conceived by Charles L'Enfant, an engineer in the Continental Army, a personal courier of Washington's during the

The Constitution

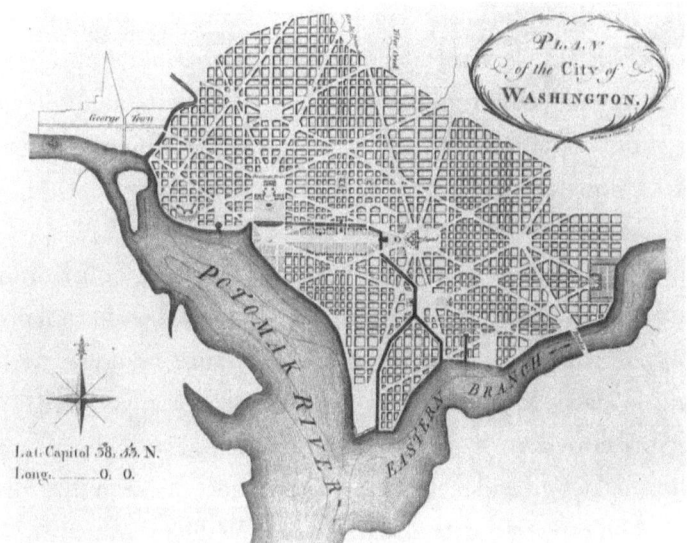

Plan of the City of Washington (Charles L'Enfant, 1792)

Revolution, and a founding member of the Society of the Cincinnati.

Jefferson and many of the Founders associated the new federal government with the model of civic virtue in the ancient Roman republic. The task of weaving that ideal into the very physicality of the new governmental seat was to Jefferson all-important. An inlet creek that ran the length of the proposed Mall from the Potomac River to the site of the main legislative building was even named the Tiber, after the river that runs through Rome. Jefferson conceived of and mediated a national design competition for the central building to house the Congress—the most important structure in the city. The contest would be judged by Washington himself, along with the commissioners of the city. Jefferson drew sketches that set a circular plan for the building and its primary chambers, pushing for a Neoclassical style of architecture over Georgian and Italian Renaissance models. For the year and a half that the competition was in progress, Jefferson worked closely with Stephen Hallett, a professional architect born in Paris and trained in England, on five different iterations of a design for the structure. He placed chief importance on working the principles of the Constitution and the Bill of Rights into the architectural and sculptural program of the building in which the legislature would write the nation's laws. In July of 1793, at Washington's suggestion, Jefferson convened a meeting in Philadelphia to choose the winning design and facilitated a compromise decision that married Hallett's fifth design with that of William Thornton, an amateur architect. On September eighteenth, Washington laid the cornerstone in a ceremony with full Masonic rites.

Jefferson hoped that "the first temple dedicated to the sovereignty of the People" would visually express the principles that formed the thought-architecture of the Constitution. In its beams and uprights, its façade, its layout and program of sculpture and ornamentation, Jefferson meant the building to be a perpetual reminder to the nation's Congress of the high office they had been granted by the people to administer the powers entrusted to them under the Constitution. On a map drawn by L'Enfant that indicated the position of the primary structures, Jefferson crossed out L'Enfant's label of the "Congress House" and inked in the name "Capitol," a reference to Rome's national temple, the temple to Jupiter Optimus Maximus, which stood on the Capitoline Hill. The American Capitol, too, would hold the central position on the highest hill, looking out over the capital city and the nation. During the architectural contest for the building's design, Jefferson proposed that the central mass be modeled after the Roman Pantheon, the temple dedicated to all the gods. So did the Capitol come to have a great dome as its outstanding feature.

There is a seventh principle of governance enshrined in the Preamble of the Constitution, one that seems an addendum or final flourish to the preceding six, but in fact stands on its own as an essential component of the Constitution's structure. The words, "for ourselves and our posterity," have been taken to mean that the framers of the Constitution intended it not only for themselves, but for future generations. The Founding Fathers made provisions for amendments to the Constitution, and those changes have often been credited for its extraordinary ability to withstand the test of time when so many others that imitated its example have failed. Jefferson's attempt to infuse Constitutional principles into the architecture of the Capitol Building suggests a deeper meaning of the seventh principle of government, often called, "the living Constitution." The transformation of a thought construct into the realm of art and architecture enlivens such thoughts, assists future generations in grasping them in a living way. Even to this day, the Capitol is known as the Temple of Liberty.

chapter six

THE FEDERALISTS

The ratification of the Constitution in 1788 set the stage for the first Presidential election. Washington received the vote of every member of the Electoral College, and four years later he was again the unanimous selection. The vote had also been unanimous when he was chosen to become the Commander-in-chief of the Continental Army and again when he was elected the President of the Constitutional Convention. To say that there was universal respect for his leadership does not capture how unusual it is that in these four elections for the highest offices in the land there was not a single dissenting vote. This phenomenon earned Washington the attribution, "first in war, first in peace, and first in the hearts of his countrymen." One philosopher-historian who lived at that time insisted that the American form of government would fail because the common man had an innate need for the idea of kingship externalized in a monarch. The first months of Washington's initial term in office seemed to confirm Hegel's pessimistic view of the American experiment in democracy. The President toured the various states in what appeared to be the "progress of a king." He visited the Northern states in the fall of 1789 and completed the process after the mid-term elections by traveling through the Southern states. By 1791 his birthday, like that of a European monarch, had become a national holiday. How such adulation did not turn his head and send him down the wrong road reflects the sincerity of his letter to Wheatley, in which he expressed his abhorrence of vanity. Washington instead took the road less traveled and ushered in the new idea of the President. King George III, meanwhile, lapsed further into madness. It was said that he imagined himself to be the second coming of Washington.

Historians often refer to those days as Washington's honeymoon, and the first days in office for many succeeding Presidents have contained the mood of joy and contentment that enveloped America in 1789. Certain petitions arrived in Congress less than a year after Washington's inauguration to dispel this mood. The first one came from the Society of Friends and demanded that Congress bring an end to slavery, which the Quakers viewed as a blot on the U.S. Constitution. The second petition, from Benjamin Franklin—the one American who shared with Washington the highest esteem of his countrymen—supported the Quakers' plea. The positions of other Founding Fathers on this issue echoed that of Franklin: Jefferson had opposed slavery from the first day that he took his seat as a member of the Virginia House of Burgesses, John Adams' opposition to slavery during the Continental Congress was notorious, and Hamilton would be instrumental in getting the New York legislature to outlaw slavery in that state. For the first and last time until the eve of the Civil War, the Senate took up debate on the question of slavery. All of the arguments, both pro and con, were offered at that time and various solutions were proposed, none of which seemed feasible. Franklin died within a year; had he lived longer, it is probable that the Senate would have done more than just debate this issue and settle at an impasse. While the Founders have been roundly criticized for leaving the problem of slavery for a later generation to solve, some have noted that the Founding Fathers had accomplished so much in their lives that to expect them to confront the one issue that threatened to tear the fragile Union asunder was unrealistic. This generation of heroes was exhausted, and the problem of slavery seemed to lack a practicable solution.

Washington's own view on this matter is worth considering, since the ideas of the proponents of these petitions—to repatriate slaves to their homeland and to reimburse slave-owners out of the public treasury—were so obviously flawed. Although Washington was a plantation owner and did not seem morally opposed to slavery, he disliked the institution of slavery. Washington was a realist. He had not labored under illusions while leading the Continental Army; rather he pursued the practical course of training a force to oppose the standing army of Great Britain. After resigning his commission in 1783, he returned to his plantation and gradually turned it into a series of farms in an effort to defeat the British economic system of mercantilism. He needed trained carpenters and masons to accomplish this task, and providing for ignorant slaves only compounded his difficulties. Washington took the position that slaves should be educated, taught a craft, and then freed to pursue their vocation. It was the one suggestion that might have led the Founders out of their dilemma. Washington again wrestled with the curse of slavery during his retirement from public office in 1797. He defeated it through his Last Will and Testament, which provided that upon Martha Washington's death, their slaves were to be freed. The will gave one slave immediate freedom—William Lee, Washington's personal valet, who was at the general's side throughout the Revolution and rode with him in battle. One year after her husband's death, Martha carried through her husband's wishes and freed both her slaves and his. The emancipation covered every one of their slaves, including the one whom Washington had brought to Philadelphia to serve as chef to the President's household and who had betrayed his trust by escaping to freedom on the last day of his second term. The slave's name was Hercules.

The second challenge to Washington's Presidency arose some months after the arguments over slavery had abated. His cabinet threatened to split over the issue of the national debt, but Washington helped to broker the deal between the Secretary of the Treasury and the Secretary of State that led to the creation of a national bank and the founding of a new capital city. How Washington could have reconciled two personalities as opposite as those of Hamilton and Jefferson and move them to a mutually agreeable solution to their passionate differences is another of the marvels of his leadership. This talent of Washington derived from his willingness to listen to all the ideas and reasoning of both participants without judgment or interjection,—a gift of silence for which Washington was famed among his contemporaries. For Franklin, in his plan of disciplined self-improvement, silence held the preeminent position among the virtues since it smoothed the way for the attainment of knowledge. For the Father of our country, it became his characteristic trait. This virtue, when viewed askance, provided ammunition for Washington's detractors, who chided him for his aloofness. It was well known among his close friends and colleagues that Washington's composure overlaid a seething temper that could burst forth in a withering torrent when he was frustrated or provoked. Like an empiricist, Washington wished to hear all of the pertinent facts of the matter at hand and then take time to deliberate on the best course of action, the same method that he had used as Commander-in-chief when he had asked for input from members of his staff. After making a decision, Washington expressed his intention with perfect clarity and expected it to be carried out. The willingness of his subordinates to follow his prescribed course of action had much to do with their feeling that all ideas had received a full hearing.

By the end of his first term, the burden of office weighed heavily on Washington and he wished to retire to private life, but Hamilton and Jefferson insisted that he run for a second term. Though he was already working on his farewell address to the nation and longing for his home at Mt. Vernon, Washington put aside his personal desires once again and acquiesced to stand for another term in office. His next years in office proved to be even more difficult than those in his first term. Despite his legendary status, Washington began to experience partisan attacks directed against him and his policies. While events such as the Whiskey Rebellion demanded that the President focus on domestic crises that threatened to tear at the fabric of government, the true threat to the Republic came from the escalating tensions between England and France. The new nation swayed in a delicate balance between her still powerful and wealthy former parent—to which she was tied by language, trade, and culture—and the nation that had helped her gain her freedom. America could not fairly afford open hostility with either. In keeping with his ideal to avoid foreign entanglements, Washington sent the Supreme Court Justice, John Jay, to England to negotiate a treaty with Great Britain under concessions designed by Hamilton to ensure an agreement. The importance of avoiding war and remaining neutral in the brewing conflict, to Washington's thinking, overrode the nuisance of the unfavorable economic terms of the Jay Treaty, which included granting Great Britain most favored nation status for purposes of trade. Jefferson saw the situation differently, even comparing Washington to Cato and quoting from Washington's favorite play: "a curse on his virtues, they have undone his country." The Jefferson partisans advocated an aggressive stance towards England, convinced that Parliament lacked the resources to declare war and that a formal treaty would weaken the Republic unfavorably by extending the powers of the central government. The storm of disagreement around the Jay Treaty was so pronounced that it instigated the formation of the two parties that would define the political landscape for the next thirty years. The course of events following the treaty's signing in 1794 would suggest that the Jeffersonians were mistaken and that Washington's virtue had indeed saved America, since the war that Washington feared would break out finally came to American shores in 1812. The lapse of eighteen years gave the young Republic time to gain the strength necessary to repel a second attack from the most powerful army on the face of the earth.

Washington left the office of President after his second

term, for no one could further gainsay his return to Mt. Vernon. This act established a precedent followed by every successor to the office until Franklin Delano Roosevelt and was finally incorporated into the Constitution through the passage of the 22nd amendment. This decision, perhaps more than any other, throws a light on Washington that illuminates the depths of his character. The world had marveled at Washington's renunciation of kingly power, but more strange still was his willingness to forsake even the Presidency. His deed reflects not a lack of ambition, but an unprecedented control over it. Resigning his commission at Annapolis in 1783, Washington had affirmed the highest ideals of the Revolution, in a single gesture repudiating kingship and allowing a republican form of government by the people to stand forth on the world stage. Thirteen years later, he established one of the sustaining principles of republican democracy by modeling the orderly transition of power in deference to the rule of law, regardless of personal interest. Washington's ability to exercise self-control and pursue a path of action directly counter to his inmost desires had served him even in wartime as he adopted a defensive strategy, continually retreating in the face of General Howe's advancing column and thereafter avoiding direct engagements when so many others clamored for an attack. There is no general of ancient times that Washington is less akin to than Fabius, the consul who led the Roman army against Hannibal but refused to engage his superior foe in open battle. Yet it was the Fabian strategy of "the Delayer" that Washington adopted. Gouverneur Morris, who knew Washington well, delivered a eulogy on this theme of the tumultuous passions that resided in Washington's soul and his extraordinary command over them. Washington's gift for the wise renunciation gave rise to the superficial view of his legendary calmness. It masked over the Herculean emotions held in check by the willingness of an Antony to sacrifice himself for the sake of his beloved.

Early in 1795 Washington had informed his cabinet of his decision to retire, and the first political campaign for President began. Profound disagreement on matters of political philosophy and governance had been commonplace from the early days of the Revolution, finding expression in the debates of the Continental Congress and the Constitutional Convention, and especially in the pointed arguments of the Federalists and Anti-Federalists during the ratification contest. With the departure of that single individual who could elicit unanimous approbation, the divisions among the Founders became deep and personal. Adams and Jefferson,—fast friends during the Revolution and through the years leading up to the Constitutional Convention,—staked out the lines of the first partisan divide. With Washington retired and Franklin dead, these two men were the preeminent candidates for leadership of the country, but they were now distant and divided, both personally and politically. Jefferson had prepared for the inevitable contest by organizing the Republican-democratic Party, and he headed his party's ticket. Adams, who had left to Hamilton the task of parrying Jefferson by founding the Federalist party, chose, in the final months of Washington's administration, to retire to his farm, where he professed indifference to the election. Washington's vice-president for two terms, Adams seemed the natural candidate for the Federalists. Yet he could not take such a step without careful deliberation and consultation with his wife, Abigail. Adams' letters to Abigail show that her virtues were the whetstone of his conscience, that she was his loadstone and pointed him to his true north. Their farm in Braintree (now Quincy), Massachusetts,—humble though it was in contrast to Jefferson's grand estate,—also had a role to play, grounding Abigail and restoring the powers of her more famous husband. John and Abigail's work in the stony, New England fields provides an unexpected meaning to the society which Washington established for his officers. Warriors not on the battlefield, but nonetheless on the front lines of an epic contest, their lives present the ideal of Cincinnatus in its most literal sense.

In the fall of 1796, Washington formally notified the whole country of his intention not to seek a third term. His farewell was not a speech delivered before an audience, but an address that he had worked on for over four years and that he gave to the newspapers for publication. Hamilton assisted with the numerous revisions, his masterful style providing both logic and power, but the content of "The Farewell Address" was Washington's. Just as Wheatley had once presented him with a great prophecy, now Washington seemed prepared to issue one of his own. He wrote of the danger of foreign entanglements and warned that Columbia must be an example for other nations, a beacon of freedom, not a participant in their disputes and wars. He also told of the danger of partisan politics and warned that self-interest must not supercede the needs of the American people as a whole. The champion of Columbia knew of her dual nature and sought to clarify the twin dangers that she would face. Washington's warnings helped illumine her ideals as well:

Peace and Liberty.

Adams was elected President in 1796, and his inauguration in 1797 gave him a hint of what was in store for him. As he waited to take the oath of office, he noticed the glance of Washington that seemed to say, "Ay! I am fairly out and you fairly in! See which of us will be the happiest." Adams fulfilled his ambition and became the second President of the United States; Jefferson would be his Vice-President. Difficulties soon beset the new administration, the foremost of which came from France. Jefferson's opposition to the Jay Treaty created political distance between himself and Adams, but it was the French Revolution that broke open a deeply personal divide in their friendship. Jefferson lauded the uprising of the French people as a sign of the awakening spread of democracy and liberty, whereas Adams saw the detestable tyranny of a bloody mob as he had once before in Boston in 1770. The French Revolution in fact produced something like the opposite of its American predecessor. The soil of democratic institutions had nurtured the growth of freedom in the States, yet it seemed only too apparent across the sea that the demand for the rights of man in the stony absence of such institutions led only to anarchy and tyranny. Perhaps more confounding, the Freemasonic lodges that had worked quietly to such great effect in supporting the freedom of their American brethren seemed to fail entirely in their own country. Jefferson's inability to recognize the danger of secret societies entering into politics out of their own self-interest (which Franklin had so carefully avoided and the Count of St. Germain had warned against) was the concomitant of his idealism, a certain species of naiveté.

The new government of France, under Napoleon, viewed the treaty with England as an act of aggression, stoking the Democratic-Republican argument that the Federalists were woefully misguided in their handling of foreign policy. Pressure to take action mounted as the French navy began raiding American ships on the high seas. Suffering under an onslaught of personal attacks in the newspapers that questioned his integrity and fitness for office, reeling from public pressure in the wake of botched negotiations with France in the XYZ affair, Adams signed the Alien and Sedition Acts into law. The Alien Act took aim at French and other foreign agents operating on American soil, giving the President power to deport any alien he considered "dangerous to the peace and safety of the United States," and the Sedition Act attempted to protect members of Congress and the administration, especially the President himself, from "false, scandalous, and malicious writing." While Adams had the good sense to make little use of the powers of these acts, so inimical were they to the Columbian ideal, he could justly have employed them against his own Vice-President. Historians generally regard Jefferson's support for France as bordering on treason. He hid numerous betrayals of the President by members of his own cabinet. Jefferson even bankrolled the libelous attacks on Adams in the press.

The French demanded that the United States desist trading with England, using its naval superiority as a goad. Adams endorsed building a fleet of warships that could challenge the French navy and protect American shipping, but he was unenthusiastic about a plan in Congress to rebuild the standing army. Hamilton broke with the President and led the Federalists in agitating for an outright declaration of war with France. Facing the opposition of both parties in Congress, Adams had little choice but to concede to the military buildup, and he called Washington out of retirement to lead the army and lend it his prestige. Washington, who was by now too old to take the field personally, agreed on the condition that Hamilton be made his second-in-command—effectively placing him at the head of the army. Adams was adamantly opposed to such a position of power for Hamilton, but his own Secretary of State and Secretary of War were secretly working against their President to ensure Hamilton's rise, and Washington insisted, even threatening to resign his commission. Adams relented. Unfortunately, Hamilton's willingness to take advantage of this opportunity made Jefferson's betrayal of the public trust seem minor. Hamilton's ambition appeared boundless, and he laid plans to use the standing army to challenge the threat posed by France by conquering the remainder of the American continent and then returning to seize control of the federal government, thereby ending what he considered a failed experiment in democracy. Abigail warned that Hamilton was touched with madness, a new Bonaparte; Noah Webster saw more to the heart of the matter, describing him as the "American Caesar." The most serious mistake that Washington made in his whole life was to entrust Hamilton with the responsibility for creating what was called the New Army. Despite Jefferson's warnings, Washington continued to turn a blind eye to Hamilton's plot to institute a military dictatorship in America. When Washington was finally confronted with proof, he renounced Hamilton's ambition, thereby preserving his legacy.

Sick at heart from the attacks against him, exhausted and isolated, Adams withdrew from the seat of government in Philadelphia in order to conduct the business of the executive branch from his home in Braintree. In the company of Abigail, he crafted the policy that led the young Republic between the twin dangers posed by Jefferson and Hamilton. Alone against his own Cabinet and both houses of Congress, he kept faith in the power of negotiation over arms and sent an envoy to sue for terms of peace with Napoleon. Adams considered the Treaty with France in 1800 to be his greatest achievement and asked that the inscription on his tombstone refer to it. This treaty ended the threat of war with France, but it cost him the support of both political parties and, ultimately, the Presidency. The news that the treaty had been signed—that Adams, in holding to the dictates of his conscience against the roar of the crowd had been right, had spared the Republic—came too late to be a factor in the bitter partisan election of 1800. The Republican-democrats triumphed, and Jefferson became the President-elect. Adams retired to his farm, surrendering to Jefferson a peaceful and prosperous nation. The treaty stood, a testament to Adams' loyalty to the ideal of peace.

The giant personality of Washington dominated the interval from the ratification of the Constitution to Jefferson's election, the period of the Federalists. The hint that Columbia's champion was the reincarnated Hercules, as the Neoclassic artists strongly suggested, casts a new light on his preeminent position and the universal adulation that he received both at home and abroad. Shakespeare's intimation that Hercules reincarnated as Marc Antony suggests that the founding of America may be related to those of the classical civilizations, that the events of the Federalist period may be prefigured in ancient Greece and Rome. The great rowing contest in the voyage of the *Argo*,—in which Hercules was defeated, and which lead the heroes to the island of Kios, where Hercules abandoned the quest and was left behind,—appeared again as Antony's defeat in the sea battle of Actium, and finally as Washington's retirement from office and his Farewell Address. As much as the smaller events reveal parallels and insights, the grand gestures tell of an epoch-making theme that advanced across civilizations, manifesting something new at each step until its unfolding in America at the close of the eighteenth century. The Federalist story did not tell of a voyage on the Argo and a search for the Golden Fleece, but of Washington and Adams steering the ship of state towards the ideal of Peace. It told not of the coming of Augustus, the man-god, who ushered in the Roman Empire, but of the people as the source of the powers of government, and of the President, not standing above the law, but carrying out his oath to the Constitution and upholding the ideal of Liberty. Always present was that spirit who had inspired the founding epics of many nations down through history, now standing forth to articulate her own high purposes and mission, and taking a hand in the birth of the United States under its first two Presidents. This story is the Legend of Columbia.

chapter seven

THE DEMOCRATS

The Democratic-republican and Federalist parties began to form well before the end of Washington's second term, but the Founders had failed to anticipate their emergence during the framing of the Constitution. As a result, the electoral process defined by the Constitution was entirely neutral on matters of party interest or prerogative. Despite the fact that Jefferson and Adams stood on opposite ends of the political spectrum, the non-partisan Electoral College chose Jefferson to be Vice-President to Adams in the election of 1796 since he had received the second highest number of votes. While serving as the presiding officer of the Senate, Jefferson made constructive use of his time and wrote the *Manual of Parliamentary Practices*, which the Senate still uses today. More importantly, he used his close proximity to both Congress and the Cabinet to consolidate political power and build a solid base of support for the next election. His long-range goal of building the Democratic-republican Party into a potent national organization rested on a strategy of bringing the common man, especially the farmer, into the political process by extending the vote to more and more people. In Aaron Burr, Jefferson found a potent ally to help with this daunting task. Burr applied his considerable legal talent (he was reputed to have never lost a case) to organizing the common laborers in New York City, who could not vote due to a requirement in the Constitution that citizens must own land in order to participate in national elections. He wrote out a series of complicated legal contracts to enable large groups of workers to make communal purchases of property, which proved key in wresting the state of New York from the Federalists. The first big-city machine, Tammany Hall, helped sweep the Democratic party to victory in the election of 1800.

While the Jefferson-Burr ticket handily defeated the Federalists, a technicality in how electors cast their votes and a botched plan for one of the Democratic electors to withhold his vote resulted in a tie. The Democratic-republican votes in the electoral college went to both Jefferson and Burr for President. Despite his protests to Jefferson himself that he had no personal investment in the Presidency and would be willing to step aside if Jefferson wished it, Burr made no motion to defer. Under election rules, the tie threw the contest for President into the House of Representatives, where Burr apparently hoped to receive enough Federalist support to deny Jefferson the high office that he had rightly won. With the Federalist-controlled states divided between the two candidates, neither could gain an absolute majority in the House, and the voting dragged on, ballot after ballot, for seven days, always with the same result. In a poignant twist, the Presidency came down to a choice by Hamilton, the leader of the Federalists, between the two men who, above all others, had thwarted his ambitions. Hamilton decided that Jefferson was the more principled candidate and began lobbying delegates to switch their votes. Finally, on the thirty-sixth ballot, the balance shifted and the majority went to Jefferson. His inaugural ceremony showed Jefferson's unassuming nature for the entire nation to see. He refused to ride in a carriage, instead riding a horse down the muddy street from the newly finished White House to the recently constructed Capitol to take the oath of office. There would be no progress of a king for the representative of the common man. Even to this day, the tradition continues that a President walk at least part of the way to his inauguration.

The purchase of the Territory of Louisiana from France in 1803 stands as the signature achievement of the first Jefferson administration. With the stroke of a pen, Jefferson doubled the size of the young nation at the cost of mere pennies per acre. His original goal in opening negotiations with the French had been fairly modest, but fortuitous circumstances brought an opportunity that not even the great proponent of limited and disciplined government could gainsay. James Monroe delivered Napoleon's offer of a vast parcel of land west of the Mississippi. In return, Napoleon asked for fifteen million dollars, money that France needed in order to shore up its treasury in the face of a renewed struggle with England. Jefferson agreed to accept the land deal since he, along with many of the other Founders, had a vision of America's future and believed that extending Columbia's boundaries to the shores of the Pacific Ocean would be an important condition for the emergence of a new Rome generations hence. Bonaparte is said to have exclaimed: "This accession of territory strengthens forever the power of the United States; I have just given to England a maritime rival that will sooner or later humble her pride."

Just as the deal with Hamilton had required Jefferson to swallow a bitter pill—the National Bank—so did the deal with Napoleon force him to compromise the very principles of good governance that he had espoused. The Louisiana Purchase contradicted Jefferson's beliefs in paying off the national debt to attain fiscal responsibility and avoiding any expansion of executive powers. He was so concerned about the legality of the purchase that when he learned it had gone through, he was certain that a constitutional amendment would be necessary in order to validate it. The cost of the Louisiana Territory was about three-quarters of the amount spent to conduct the Revolutionary War, money that had been appropriated by the Congress and was under its purview to spend. The negotiations for the purchase, conducted quickly and deftly by Jefferson's principals and agreed to without review by Congress, set a precedent and increased the authority of the executive branch at the expense of the legislative. Though Jefferson exposed himself to sharp criticism for his inconsistency, he turned his self-contradictory action to good account by limiting white settlement in the expanded territory, throwing himself into the task of exploring the newly-bought lands, and planning out the Lewis and Clark Expedition down to the last detail. Jefferson successfully transformed a likely prelude to conquest into a famous scientific expedition.

The election laws of the early republic made for strange bedfellows in the Presidency and Vice-Presidency,—Jefferson serving under Adams being a particularly contentious example. That pairing proved to be less strange than Aaron Burr's tenure in the second-highest office during Jefferson's first term in office. Jefferson had wanted James Madison on the Democratic-republican ticket with him, but Burr had maneuvered his way into the slot through power politics. More than an unlikely ally, Burr managed to adopt a contrary position to Jefferson on seemingly every issue, ultimately becoming an outcast in his own party after being in office barely a year. Toward the end of his term, his career in the federal government all but over, Burr turned his sights on the governorship of New York. Seeking to regain political power by appealing to the Federalist base in that state, he hoped to create a new majority and upset the Democratic-republican candidate. Alexander Hamilton would have none of Burr's opportunism. He had foiled Burr's bid for the Presidency and now placed himself squarely in opposition to his pursuit of the governorship. Hamilton's letters to his Federalist friends and the newspapers disparaged Burr's character and criticized his lack of principle. These attacks may not have been the deciding factor in Burr's defeat, but the Vice-President was desperate to make some sort of response to his political downfall. Word reached Burr that Hamilton had said even worse at a private gathering. He demanded that Hamilton recant the insults to his character, but Hamilton refused. In June of 1804, Burr challenged Hamilton to a duel.

For much of their lives, Hamilton and Burr's paths had crossed and re-crossed in a series of seemingly marvelous coincidences, from the time of their first meeting at Harlem Heights to that fateful day almost twenty-eight years later on a cliff overlooking the Hudson River. The significance of the intertwining destinies of the two men gained an added dimension after

Hamilton's death. Burr, accused of being a murderer and cold-blooded at that, stripped of all political and moral standing at home, dogged by warrants for his arrest even while he held the second-highest office in the land, began to nurse grandiose dreams. Finding himself without a country, he determined to form one of his own. His dreams of empire were no less magnificent than Hamilton's, though his methods were far less effectual and his chances for success more pathetic than those of the American Caesar. For the next two years, Burr attempted to build various alliances to help him carve a new nation out of the Louisiana territory and the lands that he hoped to seize from the Spanish in the Southwest. He planned to incite a conflict along the Texas frontier, imagining that it would lead to an invasion of Mexico. Whereas Hamilton had secured command of the entire United States army and a preeminent seat in the halls of power, the pinnacle of Burr's insurgency was a meager flotilla that drifted down the Mississippi River with sixty of his adherents. Betrayed to Jefferson by a member of his own circle,—the general on whom he had pinned his hopes,—Burr was brought to trial for treason in 1807. Despite Jefferson's best efforts, Chief Justice John Marshall—long a rival of the President—acquitted Burr and released him to a self-imposed exile in Europe. Once abroad, Burr's ambition continued unabated. He lobbied the governments of Great Britain and France to support his designs for carving out a nation in the American Southwest.

Hamilton and Burr embodied a significant threat to the republic—that the desire for individual glory could trump the will of the people, that the pursuit of empire could smother democratic institutions. The two men's dreams of conquest and expansion were complementary but exclusive; had they joined together, their ineffectual plots might have materialized into a genuine challenge to Columbia. Their deep-seated personal rivalry made such an alliance impossible. The possibility that Hamilton carried with him the character and destiny of Julius Caesar hints at the possible source of the enmity that placed the two at odds. Pompey the Great, one of the preeminent Roman generals of his time, extended Roman rule through conquest in the East. He became Caesar's partner in the First Triumvirate and supported its consolidation of power, even marrying Caesar's only daughter, Julia. Pompey, however, took advantage of Caesar's absence in Gaul to turn the Senate against him, wrote laws to limit his power, and tried to strip him of his armies when he returned victorious. He led his legions against Caesar's in the great battles of the civil war that culminated in Pompey's defeat at Pharsalia. Pompey's eventual assassination and beheading by agents of the king of Egypt, who sought to curry Caesar's favor by delivering the head of his enemy, was said by Plutarch to cause Caesar such grief that he turned away and burst into tears.

The duel in 1804 between Hamilton and Burr, when viewed against the backdrop of the struggle of the leaders of the First Triumvirate for ascendancy in Rome, may not be the national tragedy that the American people at that time, and many historians later, took it to be. Both leaders of the new American Republic represented ideas that Jefferson and the Democratic-republican party had struggled against, in particular the National Bank and the big city political machine. The danger to the economic independence of the American government posed by the former and the danger to the political system posed by the latter presents a reflection of the twin threats of Caesar and Pompey to the Roman Republic. Yet the circumstances surrounding the ultimate settlement of the grudge between the two men in the fatal duel suggests that America was not in genuine peril from the forces of egotism that had led to the elevation of the emperor as a demigod above the people of ancient Rome. No armies gathered for war; only seconds accompanied the principals to the dueling grounds. In his final letter, Hamilton renounced bloodshed and placed his hope in the spirit of forgiveness. Neither of their seconds could agree on who shot first. Some historians even doubt that Burr knew that Hamilton's first shot hit high in the tree branches and posit that Burr fired without intending to cause a mortal wound. Nevertheless, Burr's shot pierced Hamilton's liver and lodged in his spine, delivering the fatal blow that stained Burr's character and ended his political career. It may have also exacted a revenge that had waited nearly two millennia to unfold.

Jefferson's reelection in 1804 gave the incumbent another chance to realize his goal of "republicanizing" government, an ideal that included more than just extending the vote to the common man. In his first term in office, he had begun the process of lifting the burden of government from the shoulders of the taxpayer by cutting government expenses. Jefferson not only tried to hold the line on expenditures of Congress and spending by his own cabinet, but he personally paid the costs of entertaining foreign dignitaries, which included providing them with the finest wines available—his own. The continuation of this practice in his second term seriously depleted his financial resources and contributed to that decline in his estate which later prompted Congress to assist him by purchasing his library and establishing one of the most renowned collections of books in the world, the Library of Congress. Jefferson fulfilled the pledge that the Founders made to each other in the conclusion of the Declaration of Independence, to dedicate "our Lives, our Fortunes, and our sacred Honor" to the cause of Freedom. Washington, Adams, Franklin, Hamilton, and the rest of the Virginia Dynasty also made similar sacrifices. Whatever their differences, enmities, or grievances with each other, their fulfillment of this oath stands as a testament to the selfless nature of the Founding Fathers as they established a new republic. They were one in their sincere desire to serve Columbia rather than themselves.

Jefferson's goal of republicanizing government faced a fiscal challenge of potentially crippling proportions in his second term. The settlement of the shared debt incurred by the states in fighting the War for Independence was, after the threat of renewed war with Britain and France, the single greatest threat to the prosperity and longevity of the young nation. While America's creditors had been generous, the volatile politics of Europe and the delicacy of existing treaties and trade agreements made it almost a matter of national security that the government remain solvent and financially independent, lest it collapse under the weight of its obligations. In his first term Jefferson had cut expenses to pay off the war debt, but at the end of that term he had saddled the federal government with an equally great burden through the purchase of Louisiana. The original impetus for opening negotiations on Louisiana had, in fact, been to secure the trade route down the Mississippi in order to avoid withering export duties that would have strangled the economic health of the territories to the west of the original thirteen states. Fortunately for Jefferson, his gamble on the debt paid off and the country prospered. Foreign trade increased rapidly, and improvements of roads and bridges helped to sustain growth in internal trade as well. With public expenses falling and tax yields on trade increasing, the national budget began to show a surplus. Jefferson's fiscal policy of retiring the debt allowed the federal government to give the surplus back to the states and the citizens themselves. As the debt fell, the amount of money budgeted for interest payments against it was returned to the common man in the form of tax relief. Cutting taxes was not the first step, but rather the final step, in Jefferson's vision of the ideal of Republican government. Perhaps Thoreau expressed Jefferson's ideal most clearly when he said, "That government is best which governs least."

The close collaboration of Jefferson and Adams, which had characterized their friendship from the time of the committees of correspondence through Washington's first administration, was all but nonexistent during their own tenures as President. They became the leaders of two opposing political parties, the Democratic-republican Party and the Federalist Party, and engaged in two bitterly contested elections. What so infuriated John Adams about the election of 1800 was that Jefferson had allowed his surrogates to spread what he knew to be lies about the actions and character of his opponent. Adams nursed his grudge against Jefferson for twelve long years until, through the intervention of a mutual friend, they learned that each still held for the other a mutual respect and love. Adams broke the silence with a gift of a book and a letter seeking reconciliation. Jefferson's warm reply emphasized his wish to resume what should not have gone so long neglected, a friendship that he framed in the epic language of a voyage: "Laboring always at the same oar, with some wave ever ahead threatening to overwhelm us and yet passing harmless under our bark, we knew not how, we rode through the storm with heart and hand, and made a happy port."† Adams was quick to reciprocate on the maritime theme, harking back to his first trip across the Atlantic to France in 1778 and noting that "your Life and mine for almost half a Century have been nearly all of a Piece, resembling in the whole, mine in the Gulph Stream, chaced [sic] by three British Frigates, in a Hurricane from the North East and a hideous Tempest of Thunder and Lightning, which cracked our Mainmast, struck three and twenty Men on Deck, wounded four and killed one." "I do not remember," he wrote, "that my Feelings, during those three days, were very different from what they have been for fifty Years."‡ In this first exchange of letters, Adams could not help but exclaim about a remarkable fact, a small but telling sign of the robust strength of the nation that the two men together had built: the mail from Monticello to Quincy, which in times of their old correspondence had taken months in transit, now took only a week.

 The renewed correspondence of these friends, though at times touching on the days of their Presidencies, dwelt primarily on the period of the Revolution,—a grand philosophical

---

† 1/21/1812. *The Adams-Jefferson Letters*, ed. Lester Cappon, p.291.
‡ 2/3/1812. *Adams-Jefferson Letters*, p.294.

investigation by the collaborators, in their elder days, of the motivations and actions of their youth. The two men had been nothing less than co-conspirators in a plot against the crown. Whereas Washington was the strength and backbone of the insurgency, Jefferson and Adams were its intellect. When the Continental Congress asked Adams to draft a declaration of the reasons for separating from Great Britain, Adams turned to Jefferson and asked him to undertake the task. On the stormy evening three nights before the fourth of July, when the Congress locked its doors against spies and took up the final debate on whether or not to commit their lives to Jefferson's words, it was Adams who stood and delivered an impassioned speech for the necessity of independence that helped to dispel doubt and rally the delegates. Together, Jefferson and Adams brought a dangerous and shadowy scheme to brilliant reality.

The nature of the bond between Jefferson and Adams,— not only in the strength of their friendship but also in the circumstances that, as Adams observed, made their lives "nearly all of a Piece,"—bears a striking resemblance to that between Washington and Hamilton. Following the same threads that bound Washington and Hamilton to the figures of Antony and Caesar in ancient Rome, the leadership roles of Jefferson and Adams in the conspiracy against the crown would resemble the intrigue of Brutus and Cassius against Caesar before he could assume the mantle of kingship. In their opposition to Caesar, Brutus and Cassius often argued about the reasons and means of achieving their end. Though the too-idealistic views of Brutus always took precedence, the conspirators remained united in their aim. Plutarch offered strong evidence of Brutus' ability to organize opposition in Rome against Caesar while he was alive and even to raise all of Athens against the Second Triumvirate after Caesar had been killed. Likewise, Jefferson and Adams, Democrat and Federalist, fought to determine the political course that the new nation would follow. Yet Jefferson's talent in political organizing and maneuvering bested Adams and led to the Virginian's victory in 1800. Adams, dispirited and bitter at the abuse that he believed had been heaped upon him in a nasty campaign, retired to his farm to nurse his wounds. Brutus and Cassius shared a bond of undying friendship that helps to explain the renewed correspondence between Jefferson and Adams after their long years of silence. Shakespeare portrayed this bond in *Julius Caesar*, in the scene at Sardis. With Caesar dead, and Antony and Octavius bearing down upon them with their armies, Brutus and Cassius argued violently and almost came to blows, but joined together once more as they discovered their abiding friendship.

BRUTUS Give me a bowl of wine.
In this I bury all unkindness, Cassius.

CASSIUS My heart is thirsty for that noble pledge.
Fill, Lucius, till the wine o'erswell the cup;
I cannot drink too much of Brutus' love.

The belief of the Founding Fathers, taken up by Neoclassical artists of the time, that Washington was the American Hercules, suggests that the character and destiny of Jefferson and Adams may be prefigured not only in Rome, but in Greece as

---

† IV.iii.158-162.

well,—that the unique friendship and collaboration of the two men may have an even more ancient precedent. The most famous friendship of ancient Greece was that between Theseus, the king of Athens, and Pirithous, the great hero and Prince of the Lapiths. Plutarch recounted how Theseus "had long since been fired by the glory of Hercules, held him in the highest estimation, and was never more satisfied than in listening to any that gave account of him." Theseus took Hercules as his inspiration when he set out on the journey that led to the accomplishment of the six minor labors and ended with his arrival in Athens. He even emulated the style and appearance of Hercules, carrying a great club for his weapon, and the heroism of his exploits later in life were so great that the saying arose, "He is a second Hercules." When his father, King Aegeus, died, Theseus became leader of all of Attica, but instead of assuming the throne and the trappings of kingship, he adopted the role of the great reformer. Determined to end the petty differences and wars of the many townships, Theseus united them under a grand design of government that he had conceived, "a commonwealth without monarchy, a democracy, or people's government, in which he should only [continue] as their commander in war and the protector of their laws, all things else being equally distributed among them."‡ Theseus, the founder of democracy in Greece, and Brutus, defender of the Republic in Rome, may stand behind Jefferson's mission in America—the herald of government of the people, by the people, and for the people. The very name of the party that Jefferson founded expressed the

---

‡ *Plutarch's Lives*, "Theseus," I.4; I.19; I.15.

union of the ideals of the two classical civilizations: the Democratic-republican party. For his own part, John Adams was the spur of the Revolution, the passionate agitator and tireless advocate; he also lent his assistance to forming the new government, especially with his defense of the idea of three-folding government. This deed reflects how Pirithous always looked up to his friend and emulated his example. In the final scene of *Julius Caesar*, Antony, after his victory over Brutus and Cassius at the Battle of Philippi, called Brutus the most noble Roman of them all. Cassius held the same view in his heart.

James Madison, the fourth President of the United States, and James Monroe, the fifth, are usually referred to as Jefferson's protégés. They had served as his law clerks before the Revolution and after the war had participated in forming the Democratic-republican party. When their time arrived to stand on their own and leave the shadow of Jefferson's wing, they took turns leading the nation. Over a span of twenty-four years, Jefferson and his protégés carried out the policy of republicanizing government, a period of sustained governance under the Democrats that earned the name of the Virginia Dynasty. In their policies and style of administration, his protégés seemed to mirror Jefferson's thoughts; together they were so like a family that Madison's wife even assisted Jefferson in providing the entertainment expected of America's head-of-state. Madison's greatest achievement, writing the Constitution, showed this mirroring quality on a grand scale as he set about the task of incorporating the disparate views of a host of delegates not only into a practical tool of governance, but into a work of art. Madison later drafted the first ten amendments to the Constitution that would become the Bill of Rights, the guarantor to the common man of the limits of the power of government. It was Madison especially who joined with Jefferson to organize the watchdog societies against governmental overreaching and Hamilton's centralizing policies, societies that became the seeds of the Democratic-republican party. Madison continued to demonstrate this remarkable capacity throughout his career, first as floor manager and leader of the opposition party in the House of Representatives, later as Jefferson's Secretary of State and principal advisor through both of his friend's terms in office. Though Madison served faithfully at Jefferson's side for over two decades and could rightly claim responsibility as a leading force in the practical creation of the new government and the realization of Jeffersonian principles in government, historians tend to deny him credit for his considerable talent and favor Jefferson. Madison does not stand as the equal to his mentor, but on a lower tier in the ranks of the Founding Fathers, below that of Adams and Jefferson.

Madison received his opportunity to leave his mentor's shadow when Jefferson stepped down at the end of his second term and handed the reigns of government to his old friend. Though much of Jefferson's tenure had been marked by peace and economic prosperity, Madison inherited a crisis that was brought on by the continuing war between Britain and France. Madison found himself in much the same difficult situation between the two warring empires that John Adams had faced when he took office after Washington's second term. Unable to oppose the great armies of France or the indomitable navy of the British, the Madison administration had only the economic bludgeon of embargo to use in defense of its claim to the privileges of neutrality. Yet the policy of nonintercourse caused economic depression at home and won no concessions from the British, who continued to raid American shipping and impress her crewmen into service aboard vessels of the Royal Navy. Madison was left with little choice if he was to defend Columbia's rights against her rivals and salvage her prosperity at home. In June of 1812, just months after Adams and Jefferson resumed their correspondence, Congress declared war on Great Britain.

British armies invaded America again as Washington had foreseen, and Madison was at the helm to repel the Redcoats a second time. The fact that this war is called the War of 1812 is indicative of a general tendency to diminish Madison's administration. Madison's critics among his contemporaries, as well as historians of a later time, took to mocking Madison for fleeing the nation's capital and suffering the disgrace of British troops burning both the White House and the Capitol Building, just as they had belittled Jefferson when, as governor of Virginia, he had fled before the forays of John Bull's army. To bolster their argument for Madison being an ineffectual President, the same critics point out that the boundaries of America were left unchanged and that the causes of the war,—the impressment of sailors and interference with trade,—were not even addressed in the Treaty of Ghent, which ended thirty months of fighting. John Adams, in a letter to Jefferson, took the opposite view, that Madison "has acquired more glory, and established more Union, than all his three Predecessors, Washington, Adams, and Jefferson, put together."† Were the War of 1812 understood as a repetition of the Revolutionary War, then might Adams' assess-

THE DEMOCRATS

Peace of Ghent 1814 and Triumph of America (Engraving, Mme. Plantou, 1820)

ment be credited and Madison receive his due. Even Hegel, the philosopher who developed the idea of repetition in history, failed to grasp the significance of the new Idea that had dawned in America in 1776. He, like the multitude of scoffers on the continent of Europe and in the British Parliament, required a confirmation of the new American Idea through a Second War for Independence. Artists of the time saw a different background to this war, one that agreed more with Adams than with later historians. They pointed to spiritual forces that had stirred the hearts of those Founding Fathers who withstood the onslaught of Britannia a second time. "The Peace of Ghent and Triumph of America," painted by Plantou in 1815 to commemorate the

---

† 2/2/1817. *The Adams-Jefferson Letters*, p.508.

treaty, showed Hercules again victorious and Columbia on her way to the Temple of Liberty, which remained unsullied by the British attack.

Along with many of his fellow Founders, George Washington looked up to the Romans not only for models of government, but for exemplars of character. In particular, he tried to emulate Marcus Cato, the second Roman of that name, usually referred to as Cato the Younger. Washington loved to see Addison's play, "Cato," and even had it performed during his time of greatest trial, while his army was in winter quarters at Valley Forge. Cato was the embodiment of Stoicism for the ancient Romans, the great student of Plato who most fully realized in earthly life the ideal of Socrates. Cato was also the father-in-law of Brutus, who had made significant strides in own his studies as well. The Stoicism of Brutus provides context for Jefferson's ambitious plan of study, which, as he outlined in his *Autobiography*, involved twelve hours of study per day and lasted for twelve years. The selfsame principles of Stoicism appear in the Jefferson's virtues: his sense of duty to society and the Republic, his calmness in the midst of political storms, his love of solitude and study, the logic and reason in his political and scientific writings, and his belief in conscience and the common man.

After following Washington's precedent in stepping down from the nation's highest office after two terms, Jefferson turned his energies away from politics and towards his interests in history, philosophy, science, agriculture, architecture, and education. As he wrote to Adams, "I have given up newspapers in exchange for Tacitus and Thucydides, for Newton and Euclid;

and I find myself much the happier."† Jefferson's conviction that an educated citizenry is the bulwark of democracy can be found in his "Bill for the More General Diffusion of Knowledge," which sought to establish a uniform system of public education in Virginia in 1778, financed at the general expense and open to all people "without regard to wealth, birth or other accidental condition or circumstance."‡ The idea of founding a university supported by public finances occurred to Jefferson as early as 1800. His university was at last chartered by the State of Virginia in 1819. Built upon land donated by James Monroe, the University of Virginia held its first classes in 1825. With Madison's assistance, Jefferson had served as its architect, had formed its curriculum, and had chosen its faculty. When it opened its doors, it rivaled the famous universities of Europe for excellence in education. Jefferson's earlier attempts to reform the educational institutions in America had been ineffective. The tendency of such institutions to hew to a religious creed and create academic traditions stifled what he deemed to be the goal of education, to provide true knowledge of history as the best protection against tyranny. The aim of education in a democratic society, he believed, was to prepare the people to receive and guard "the sacred deposit of the rights and liberties of their fellow citizens." Founding the University of Virginia was his final effort to meet this need in a comprehensive way. "This institution," he wrote, "will be based on the illimitable freedom of the human mind. For here we are not afraid to follow truth wher-

---

† 1/21/1812. *The Adams-Jefferson Letters*, p.291.
‡ *Thomas Jefferson: Writings*. Library of America, 1984. p.365.

ever it may lead, nor to tolerate any error so long as reason is left free to combat it."† Nearly half a century had to pass before Jefferson could develop his own experience of the self-evident truths in the Declaration of Independence into a pathway for others. Founding the University of Virginia became his crowning achievement.

Soon after the University of Virginia opened, Jefferson succumbed to a long illness that lasted into the summer of 1826. On July third Jefferson felt himself slipping over the threshold of death. In a final exertion of will, he clung to life through the night and into the morning that he might welcome Independence Day a last time. He breathed his last at one o'clock in the afternoon. That same morning, John Adams awoke in good health and good spirits, looking forward to a lecture he had been invited to give that evening. Close on the heels of Jefferson's death, he experienced a sudden and rapid decline. He died at 4:30 in the afternoon. The last words to pass his lips expressed the conviction that Thomas Jefferson yet lived. One legend of Theseus relates how he and Pirithous traveled to the Underworld to win Persephone as a bride for Pirithous, and how they fell before the power of Hades. The might of Hercules freed Theseus, but Pirithous had to remain behind. Similarly, Brutus and Cassius were joined in death on the field of battle at Phillipi as the armies of Octavius and Antony surrounded them—Cassius by the hand of his servant with the very sword that had slain Caesar, Brutus by falling on his own sword. In 1754, Franklin inaugurated the American Idea with the Albany Plan, and a suc-

---

† *The Writings of Thomas Jefferson*, Albert Ellery Burgh, ed. 1905. Volume 15.303.

cession of heroes rallied to the standard of freedom. In 1826, the twin deaths of the men who had assisted in giving this Idea its proper form,—of Adams, who closed the Federalist period in peace, and Jefferson, who took the central role in leading the Virginia Dynasty,—marked the culmination of the final stage of the Legend of Columbia. This seventy-two-year period, the length of a human life, came to an end in the peaceful deaths of the two captains who served as helmsmen on the ship-of-state. The marvel of this coincidence filled the American people with awe. The countrymen of Jefferson and Adams sensed the presence of Columbia as her stalwarts, the best of friends, died on her fiftieth birthday. Her twin missions of peace and freedom were emblazoned for the entire nation to see.

chapter eight

THE TEMPLE OF LIBERTY

The Freemasonic tradition that members of their order constructed the cathedrals of Europe,—those temples of incomparable architectural beauty that both inspired and expressed a profound experience of medieval Christianity,—lends a deeper significance to the time and effort that Jefferson and Washington lavished on the project of erecting the Capitol Building. The first reference to this building as the Temple of Liberty probably occurred in 1795 in a pamphlet published first in French and then translated for publication in American newspapers. Even today it has retained that appellation. From the laying of its cornerstone by Washington in 1793 to its completion in 1916, the Capitol went through repeated phases of building, renovation, partial collapse, and even destruction. During the War of 1812, the British army burned down the Capitol, an event that no more defeated America than the capture of Philadelphia had ended the Revolutionary War. Abraham Lincoln completed one of the key tasks of rebuilding the Capitol in 1863 by erecting the great iron dome that crowns the building and the statue of Liberty that stands above it. He urged the work forward even while the Civil War raged throughout the land.

On the fiftieth anniversary of the ratification of the Constitution, Lincoln delivered an address on the "Perpetuation of Our Political Institutions" in which he spoke of the importance of the Founding Fathers and of how a new generation must take up their mission. "They *were* the pillars of the temple of liberty," he intoned; "and now, that they have crumbled away, that temple must fall, unless we, their descendants supply their place with other pillars, hewn from the solid quarry of sober reason." Lincoln closed his address with the idea that the true building materials of this newly formed temple would be formed of pure thought, reason, molded "into *general intelligence, sound morality*, and in particular, a *reverence for the constitution and laws*."[†] The idea of self-development that lies at the heart of Lincoln's speech suggests a further refinement of the concept of building the Temple, one prefigured in the goal of the great esoteric leader of the European lodges. The Count of St. Germain worked towards the goal of transforming the very character of the Freemasons. In a certain sense, the effort to find the Temple of Liberty,—the epic journey undertaken, the arduous trials endured, the purity of character and motive required to enter its presence,—recalls the medieval legends of the Knights of the Round Table. This endeavor of succeeding generations to find the Temple of Liberty resembles Percival's search for Castle Carbonek, the Grail Castle.

Washington's primary focus during the final three years of his life, after he finally entered into the retirement that he had

---

[†] "Address to the Young Men's Lyceum of Springfield, Illinois." *Abraham Lincoln: Speeches and Writings, 1832-1858*. Library of America, 1989. p.36.

so long desired, was called the Potomac Project. The project represented a further evolution of his impulse to transform Mt. Vernon, though now Washington sought to create not the ideal estate, but a new city. What Franklin had achieved by turning Philadelphia into a world-class city, Washington hoped to raise from an untamed wilderness. The Potomac Project involved the transformation of the principles of the Constitution into the Capitol building as the embodiment of the new political order, but it also included the L'Enfant Plan. Charles L'Enfant,—former engineer in the Continental Army, personal courier to Washington during the Revolution, and founding member of the Society of the Cincinnati,—systematically laid out the new capital with its radial pattern for the principal streets and avenues and indicated the location of certain buildings and monuments that were to form the heart of this beautiful city. He placed the Capitol on a hill at the eastern end of the east-west axis of what has become Washington, D.C.'s most renowned tourist attraction, the Mall. He envisioned an equestrian statue to Washington being built at the western end of this axis, but President Washington, with this typical distrust of all projects that involved glorifying his accomplishments, opposed it. Following Washington's death, numerous proposals were made to create a fitting memorial to the general and President, including sculptural groups to Washington in the center of the Capitol and even a suggestion that his body be disinterred from Mt. Vernon and placed in a crypt beneath the dome. None of the schemes bore fruit until a contest in the 1830s produced a new design. In 1848, construction began on a 555-foot-tall monument, though labor shortages and other obstacles delayed its completion until 1884. The Washington Monument is an obelisk of granite, marble, and sandstone that dominates the landscape, and Congress passed a law to ensure that it would always remain the tallest structure in the city named for the first President. The north-south axis of the L'Enfant plan for the heart of Washington, D.C., lies slightly to the west of the Washington Monument. The White House,—which in 1800 was the first of the great buildings on the Mall to be completed,—stands at its northern end. Historians have offered many views of the symbolic meaning of the White House, but the interpretation most in accord with the ideas of Freemasonry would be that it stands for the lodge of the white brotherhood, those spiritual leaders of mankind who are called in the East by the name of bodhisattvas. Their foremost representative was believed to be the Count of St. Germain.

The heart of the L'Enfant plan was the large triangle formed by the vertices of the Capitol Building, the monument to Washington, and the White House. The Freemasonic brotherhoods that built these structures made sure that the cornerstones were laid with the proper Masonic rituals. Washington himself laid the cornerstone of the Capitol, while Georgetown Lodge No. 9 laid the cornerstone for the White House. Benjamin French, attired in the Masonic apron worn by Washington in 1793, conducted the ceremony to lay the cornerstone of the Washington Monument. David Ovason, in *The Secret Architecture of Our Nation's Capital*, attempted to clarify the spiritual significance of the locations of these three buildings for the Masonic groups that stood behind their construction. Ovason demonstrated that the placement of these buildings and monuments corresponds to the position of three first-magnitude stars during late summer. A kind of occult astronomy enabled the Masonic leaders to accomplish what Ovason suggested should be called the Washington Plan. The triangle in the celestial sphere bounded by Regulus, Spica, and Arcturus finds its reflection on the earthly plane. Bounded by the placement of the Capitol, the Washington Monument, and the White House, the Federal Triangle draws the forces of the constellation of Virgo, enclosed by the heavenly triangle, into the Territory of Columbia. The Federal Triangle thereby nourishes with heavenly forces, as it were, the earthly home of the guiding spirit of the nation.

The architectural design of each of the three structures reveals a further aspect of their meaning for the Masons who built them. The Washington Monument is the tallest masonry structure in the world, a monument of sheer will. Horatio Greenough said of it that it speaks but one word: "Here!" In terms of Freemasonry, it is the pillar of strength. Washington's apotheosis, that idea he had shunned while alive, points to the role that he would play after death. The connection that his contemporaries found between Washington and Hercules prefigures the Masonic meaning of this monument, since the ancient Greeks called Hercules the god of strength. The White House symbolizes the White Lodge, the dwelling place of the masters of wisdom. In Masonic terms it is the pillar of wisdom. The Capitol building was Jefferson's attempt to bring the Temple of Liberty into outward manifestation, to reveal the principles of the Constitution in its architectural forms. The statue of Columbia that was placed atop the iron dome of the Capitol stood outside of her temple rather than within, a departure from the designs of the master builders of the Parthenon and other classic temples, who envisioned their creations as dwelling places for the spiritual beings they invoked. Outside of the Capitol, the goddess seems at once to point upwards to the temple that has risen from the flames of the old Capitol, now hidden from sight, and to look upon the broad avenues that radiate from her seat out into the furthest reaches of her domain. Together the Washington Monument, the White House, and the Capitol Building, arising throughout the course of the nineteenth century, recall that high purpose which formed the content of the earliest memory of John Adams: the three pillars of Freemasonry,—the pillars of strength, wisdom, and beauty,—journeying over the Atlantic, finding a home in America, and completing the Great Circle.

A comprehensive plan for the development of the Mall and the modernization of Washington, D.C. arose at the beginning of the twentieth century and took over forty years to complete. The city planners, architects, and sculptors who took charge of this project saw themselves as restoring the L'Enfant plan, which had been obscured by overbuilding and neglect in the latter half of the nineteenth century, and renewing the Neoclassical impulse that had been active at the time of the Founding Fathers. While the Army Corps of Engineers finished the work of filling in the tidal flats around the Mall in 1900, the American Institute of Architects held a convention in the capital and invited proposals for the use of this new land. The following year Congress founded the Senate Park Commission with Daniel Burnham as its chairman. A decade earlier in

A Sanctuary for the Rights of Mankind

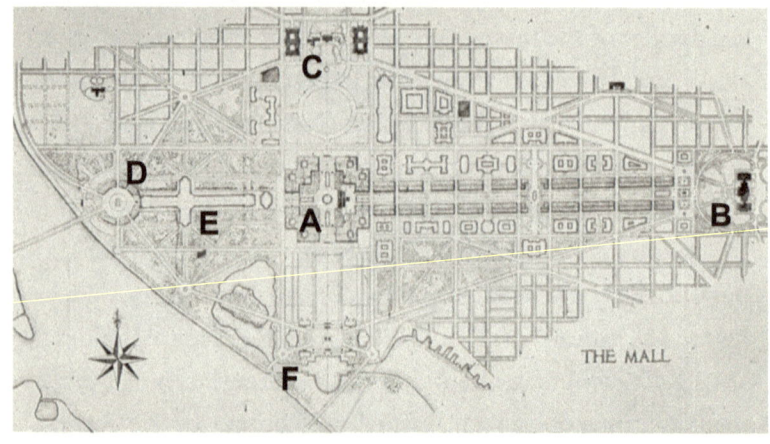

Andrew Jackson Downing's diagram of the Mall, restoring the L'Enfant Plan. (1902)

A - *Washington Monument (1884)*
B - *The Capitol (1793-1863)*
C - *The White House (1800)*
D - *Site of the Lincoln Memorial (1922)*
E - *Reflecting Pool*
F - *Site of the Jefferson Memorial (1943)*

Chicago, Burnham had held a similar position and supervised the design and construction of the various buildings housing the exhibits for the World's Columbian Exposition of 1893. The White City and its harmonious group of buildings, based on the principles of Neoclassicism, began the City Beautiful movement, which exercised a dominant influence over American architecture for the next half century. The heart of the White City was the Court of Honor designed by Charles McKim. The Agriculture Building, which covered the entire southern side of the Court of Honor, had the Temple of Ceres at its center with her statue at its apex, the only statue executed by the Exposition's chief of sculpture, Saint-Gaudens. The idea behind the design of the Court of Honor was similar to the one that had impelled

"The Republic," Court of Honor, The White City. (Daniel Chester French, 1893)

L'Enfant and Washington to orient the Federal Triangle toward the constellation of Virgo. In the Territory of Columbia, the purpose was to point to the Temple of Liberty, but in Chicago the goal was to extol the goddess herself. The centerpiece of the Court of Honor was the masterpiece of Daniel French, to whom Saint-Gardens had assigned the most important of the hundreds of sculptural exhibits for the exposition honoring Columbia. His statue was called the "Republic" and, at times, "Liberty."

When Burnham selected the other members of the Senate Park Commission, he included his collaborators from the White City and supported McKim's idea that L'Enfant's vision be renewed, and that Neoclassicism serve as the unifying principle for the Mall. The commission proposed a monument to

Lincoln west of the Washington Monument and another memorial to the Founding Fathers south of the Washington Monument and beyond the tidal reservoir. In order to implement the commission's recommendations, the Commission of Fine Arts was established in 1910, again with Burnham as chairman. It was he who selected the site for the Lincoln Memorial and its architect, Henry Bacon, who had executed several designs for the White City. By 1910 Bacon had followed Charles McKim's advice and had started his own architectural firm. Bacon's connection to the Freemasonic tradition manifested in his service as architect of the Scottish Rite Masonic Temple in Washington, D.C., as well as the keystone building of the Federal Triangle, the National Archives. His fame, however, rested on his mastery of the Greek style of architecture, and he chose one of the wonders of the ancient world, the Parthenon, to be his chief model for the Lincoln Memorial. The Parthenon had a statue of Pallas Athena within its columns and the talisman of Greece's glory—the Palladium—hidden below in the sanctuary, where her initiates practiced her rites. The Lincoln Memorial was to have a statue of a man, Abraham Lincoln. Daniel French, who had already gained distinction for his Minute Man statue in Concord and his statue of Columbia in Chicago and who had worked for Bacon on over fifty previous projects, was chosen to carve the sculpture that proved to be his greatest achievement. Though French became famous for his depiction of Lincoln, his own view of the monument gave all the credit to Bacon. French believed Henry Bacon to have been born for the sole purpose of creating the Lincoln Memorial.

  Construction on this long, horizontal building did not

begin until 1915, and not until 1922 was it open for visitors. Bacon's architecture and the Reflecting Pool that stretches out before the memorial invoke an awe and reverence that draw the visitor into its fold as if into the precincts of a temple. Its most distinguishing feature is in the center section, the statue of Lincoln that seems to call visitors to it and even encourages them to touch it. The two side sections with the paintings of Jules Guerin help to capture the mood of the Great Emancipator. These sections also contain plaques of "The Gettysburg Address" and the "Second Inaugural." In the period of the tyrannical abuses, the voice of Columbia had spoken through her orators. The child, Independence, had declared the truth of equality to the world and had founded a new nation through Jefferson's words. The speeches of Lincoln in the side sections of his memorial show that her voice helped preserve the Union as well. The placement of the Lincoln Memorial at the end of the Mall and facing the Capitol Building suggests that it is a counterpart of the Capitol, an American Parthenon that celebrates the apotheosis of the man who once spoke of becoming a pillar of the Temple of Liberty and who represents the heart and feeling life of the human being as fully as Washington signifies the will power and volitional life. Bacon's intent was surely in line with those Masons who stood behind the Washington Monument. His creation of a counterpart to the Capitol building, a new pillar of beauty, equaled the majesty of the obelisk that stands between them.

In 1934 Congress formed the Thomas Jefferson Memorial Commission. Fiske Kimball, the noted Jefferson scholar and restorer of Monticello, insisted that the memorial to Jefferson be of the same size and importance as those to Lincoln and Washington. Since the second recommendation of the Senate Park Commission,—to build a monument to the south of the Washington Monument,—had not yet been realized, the Jefferson Memorial Commission pressed for that site as the location of the new memorial. There was no competition for architectural design. The Commission selected John Russell Pope, the last living member of the City Beautiful Movement and the architect who had finished second to Bacon in 1910. Pope took the Roman Pantheon as his chief model for the Jefferson Memorial. When Pope died in 1937, his partner, Otto Eggers, carried out his design. The completion of the Memorial in 1943 signaled the end of the period of Classic Eclecticism, a final expression of the school of artists and architects who had carried the inspiration of the White City from Columbia's fair out to the rest of the nation. It also completed the triad of monuments that brought the influences of the three great classical civilizations into the Mall: the Egyptian (Washington's obelisk), the Greek (Lincoln's Parthenon), and the Roman.

The distinguishing feature of the Jefferson Memorial is its dome, modeled after the great dome that crowns the Roman Pantheon. Michelangelo had used this model for the dome of the Sistine Chapel, where it symbolized the dome of heaven. Jefferson himself had put forward the dome of the Pantheon as the template for the central mass of the Capitol Building. It was an unusual and bold suggestion since domes for centuries had been reserved for religious buildings, but one that made perfect sense to mark the principal building of the new belief in liberty that had arisen in America. Just prior to his death, Jefferson requested that his epitaph include his three most important achievements. In addition to the Declaration of Independence, Jefferson also wished to be recognized for the Statute for Religious Liberty, which had passed the Virginia legislature in 1786 and provided the legal basis for freedom of religion. The Pantheon in ancient Rome was a symbol of such freedom, a temple dedicated to all the gods that brought the different religions of the Empire together in harmony. Jefferson's statute also protected the American Republic through the separation of church and state. Two of the three men honored in the Washington Mall, Jefferson and Lincoln, were not members of any church. Jefferson's own religion remains a mystery, but the Stoicism of Brutus perhaps gives a hint of the development of reason that Jefferson deemed possible. The self-directed plan of study that he pursued at age eighteen matured into the self-evident truths of reason that he expressed at age thirty-three. The course of study that he offered at the age of eighty-two, when the University of Virginia opened its doors, was the third great achievement that he asked be recorded on his tombstone. This deed coincided with his final achievement as an architect. Jefferson used the Roman Pantheon as his model for the rotunda of the University of Virginia. In this context, it is a symbol of the human head. The University of Virginia stands for Jefferson's fervent belief that the common man, through education, can become the bulwark of the American Republic.

Pope's use of the model of the Pantheon combined both meanings. In one of its aspects it points to a fundamental freedom guaranteed in the first amendment, freedom of religion. The dome of heaven encompasses all the different religions of the world, and the American Pantheon symbolizes the respect that each citizen should naturally give to the religious beliefs of his fellow Americans. Pope's architecture seems to invite to the visitor to contemplate the Jefferson Memorial from afar. Visitors tend not to linger around it, but to contemplate it across the vistas of the Mall. This religious element unites with the other freedoms of the first amendment when a visitor enters the Jefferson Memorial and comes upon the eighteen-foot-high statue of the third President and reads the passages from the Declaration of Independence and others of his writings carved on the wall panels. Jefferson's words set thinking into motion and make apparent the need for the additional freedoms of speech, press, assembly, and petition. As the Washington Monument points to will power and the Lincoln Memorial to the feeling life, the Jefferson Memorial stands for human thinking in all its glory. It unites the man of faith and the man of reason. Its location at the southern end of the north-south axis of the Mall makes it the counterpart of the White House at the northern end. The American Pantheon, which celebrates the apotheosis of Jefferson, thus stands as the new pillar of wisdom.

The restoration of the L'Enfant plan in the twentieth century added two memorials to the Federal Triangle and transformed it into a diamond-shaped figure that enclosed the great span of the Washington Mall. The artistic unity of the Mall depends not only upon the architectural splendor of each building and monument, but on the geometry of their locations as well. This unparalleled unity also includes what seems to flow among the structures, to fill the space between. The Freemasons who had charge of the design designated this element with the term, "a spiritual stream." Franklin's discovery of the Gulf Stream, that river of warm water flowing in the ocean's depths from America to England gives a sense of the movement and purpose of such a stream, as does the later discovery of rivers of air, such as the Jet Stream, in the world's atmosphere. A spiritual stream is necessarily a metaphor, since there is no physical counterpart for what the words describe. Just as scientists can detect rivers of water and air and describe the quality and effect of their presence or absence, so can persons gifted with a particular sensitivity of perception observe a spiritual stream. Poets and artists often describe their experience of such streams as an elevated sense of a power that flows through nature, animating and uniting all things that it touches. William Wordsworth related his experience of such a stream in his poem, "Lines Composed Above Tintern Abbey."

> And I have felt
> A presence that disturbs me with the joy
> Of elevated thoughts; a sense sublime
> Of something far more deeply interfused,
> Whose dwelling is the light of setting suns,
> And the round ocean and the living air;
> And the blue sky, and in the mind of man;
> A motion and a spirit, that impels
> All thinking things, all objects of all thought,
> And rolls through all things.

Emerson related a similar experience in his book *Nature*: "Standing on the bare ground,—my head bathed by the blithe air and uplifted into infinite space,—all mean egotism vanishes. I become a transparent eyeball; I am nothing; I see all; the currents of the Universal Being circulate through me; I am part or parcel of God."

The designers and builders of the five principal monuments and buildings on the Mall worked to imbue them with a magnificenct presence that would inspire feelings of awe and reverence in the visitor, preparing a mood appropriate to communicate the spiritual significance not only of what the Founders and the Guardians of the Republic had done in the past, but to suggest its continued activity in the present. This mood, shared by millions of visitors every year, is the initial experience of the inward, or spiritual, architecture of the Mall, a feeling, as it were, of entering the antechamber to the Temple of Liberty. The spiritual streams that unite the five buildings and monuments of the Washington Mall have been described by a spiritually-gifted individual, a man who has written many books on the spiritual background of the earthly environment and who was chosen by his native Slovenia to design its national flag. Upon his first visit to Washington, D.C., in the spring of 2004, Marko Pogacnik entered the Washington Mall from its western end near the Lincoln Memorial. He noticed a stream of spiritual guidance flowing towards him, passing over the Washington Monument and diving down as it crossed over the Lincoln Memorial. It joined with two other spiritual streams in the rear of the Memorial. The first of these other streams was an etheric stream of life forces or elemental beings that came from the northwest and seemed to flow out of the Potomac River, which defines the western boundary of the Mall before continuing on its course down to the Atlantic Ocean. The second stream was an astral stream of soul forces from "the ancestors" that came from the southwest and seemed to flow across the bridge from

Arlington National Cemetery, where lie the bodies of those who had given their lives in Lincoln's War. The three streams of the elementals, the ancestors, and spiritual guidance merged into one and emerged from the front of the Lincoln Memorial as a huge tube of light, many feet in diameter. This stream traveled over the Reflecting Pool, through the Washington Monument, and on into the Capitol.

When Mr. Pogacnik walked down the Mall toward the Capitol, he also noticed a smaller stream issuing from the Lincoln Memorial and moving diagonally to the Jefferson Memorial where it turned to follow the north-south axis. It traveled across the Mall and into the White House, where it turned again to move diagonally down Pennsylvania Ave. It then entered the Capitol Building and united again with the larger stream. Thus were the three pillars, the monuments to the three great American Presidents, joined with the White House and the Capitol in the vision of Marko Pogacnik. Spiritual streams wove together all five elements of the restored L'Enfant' plan.

Nearing the Capitol itself, Mr. Pogacnik discerned a spiritual chamber that seemed to float above the statue of Columbia that crowns the dome. There appeared to his spiritual sight a vision of the Founding Fathers within. There he beheld the Temple of Liberty itself, the source of the stream of spiritual guidance and the spiritual counterpart of the first Capitol building burned in 1814. When he turned toward the Capitol building, he discerned smaller spiritual streams raying outward along the avenues that L'Enfant had laid out, journeying to the northwest, southwest, northeast, and southeast. These streams, deriving from the spiritual stream of Freemasonry or Rosicru-

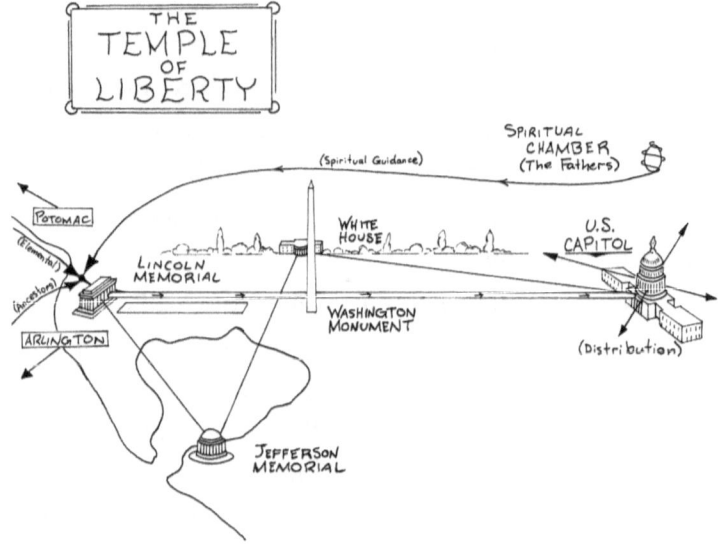

cianism, extended outwards to the four corners of the country and even the world. They can be said to contain the spiritual guidance of the Fathers, intentions that have served to inspire those souls who are atuned to them. Lincoln maintained that a proper interpretation of the Constitution was one in accord with these intentions. He carefully shaped his own personal horror of slavery into a policy that he felt best reflected the Founders' hope that future generations would solve the problem they had not been able to confront, that their fellow citizens would find a way to constrain or even extinguish slavery. The Founders created the Constitution, not as an object for perpetual observance, but as an initial foundation for something that would continue to unfold anew in future generations. The Rosicrucian stream points to the profound depth of the seventh principle of the American form of government, the Living

Constitution.

The above diagram, which Mr. Pogacnik drew the following day, was the result of a bodily vision, a heightened awareness and sensitivity experienced through the physical senses. The fact that this vision presented spiritual facts and beings in spatial dimensions indicates that it was more in the form of an hallucination than a genuine Imagination, more of a preparatory event than a true experience of the Idea itself, as Plato or Emerson would call it. Neither should the vision of the Fathers in the spiritual chamber be taken to mean that the actual individualities of the Founders were present. Rather, it implies that the band of brothers had so transformed their character, as the Count of St. Germain had wished, that the resultant spiritual product might remain behind in the earthly sphere after their spirits had crossed over the threshold of death and ascended to further realms. This perfection of character defines "apotheosis," the term used by Neoclassic artists to explain the transformation that Washington and Franklin had accomplished in order to join Liberty in her temple. Such perfection is also at the heart of Lincoln's speech at the Lyceum in Springfield on "The Perpetuation of Our Political Institutions." The Freemasonic practice of the virtues, so clearly stated by Franklin, and the devotion to knowledge, so fully exemplified by Jefferson, join with the study of the Constitution, so deeply grasped by Lincoln. All three paths lead to the ideal of becoming a pillar in the Temple of Liberty.

A higher level of vision might discover what Mr. Pogacnik did not see, a spiritual counterpart to the statue of Columbia that stands atop the Capitol Building, a manifestation of the goddess herself within the inner sanctum of the Temple of Liberty attending the Founders, as she so often did in Neoclassic representations of her. The indications and hints for how one might approach Columbia were once woven into the very cultural fabric of America. Columbia's presence and influence was abroad in the popular consciousness from the latter half of the eighteenth century through the third quarter of the nineteenth, as witnessed in the great outpouring of poetry, music, sculpture, and art dedicated to her and to the principles and ideals that she championed. The genuine inspiration of a poet such as Phillis Wheatley could envision her activity in the individuals and events of the times and describe them in such a way that her countrymen recognized their truth. Towards the end of the nineteenth century, Columbia seemed to withdraw. She retreated from the poet's pen and disappeared from the artist's brush and the sculptor's chisel. Her anthem was replaced by another as the national song, and her likeness disappeared from the nation's coinage. The reason for this gradual withdrawal appeared in a poem by Walt Whitman, "By Blue Ontario's Shore," in which the poet held a dialog with Columbia,—whom he variously called America, Liberty, and Mother,—about the past and future of the People of the States. In the course of the poem, Whitman observed how after the Civil War Columbia ceased her involvement in the affairs of the nation, handing responsibility to the citizens themselves, as it were. He saw her "at last refuse to treat but directly with individuals." For those who yet wished to approach her, he described a necessary road of self-development and study in order to hone the character and virtue of the supplicant. In the poem, Whitman also spoke of his own future role as the guardian of the Temple of Liberty. He viewed his task as meeting those who wished to serve her and questioning them:

> He shall surely be question'd beforehand by me with many and stern questions.
> Who are you indeed who would talk or sing to America?
> Have you studied out the land, its idioms and men?
> Have you learn'd the physiology, phrenology, politics, Geography, pride, freedom, friendship of the land? Its substratums and objects?
> Have you consider'd the organic compact of the first day of the first year of Independence, sign'd by the Commissioners, ratified by the States, and read by Washington at the head of the army?
> Have you possess'd yourself of the Federal Constitution?

Whitman also pointed to one higher than himself, a Poet, whom he would one day serve as a guide. It was this Poet whom Whitman envisioned as writing the future masterwork, often called the great American novel, that would grant the American people, and even the whole world, entrance to the Temple of Liberty. Whitman saw that what, in the present, could only occur through individual effort in the form of meditation on the Constitution and the development of compassion for all the different people of this nation would, in the future, become possible for the myriads who would read the Poet's song. Through the power of poetry, the inspiration that once awoke the Sons of Liberty would again be heard throughout the land. Emerson too foretold this sublime event:

---

† "By Blue Ontario's Shore." *Leaves of Grass*, p.477.

The poet will shove all usurpers from their chairs, by electrifying mankind with the right tone, long wished for, never heard. The true center appearing, all false centers are suddenly superceded, and grass grows in the Capitol.

Appendix

TO HIS EXCELLENCY GENERAL WASHINGTON

[Below is the letter and poem Phillis Wheatley sent to General Washington at his Headquarters in 1775]

SIR,

I Have taken the freedom to address your Excellency in the enclosed poem, and entreat your acceptance, though I am not insensible of its inaccuracies.

Your being appointed by the Grand Continental Congress to be Generalissimo of the armies of North America, together with the fame of your virtues, excite sensations not easy to suppress. Your generosity, therefore, I presume, will pardon the attempt. Wishing your Excellency all possible success in the great cause you are so generously engaged in. I am,

Your Excellency's most obedient humble servant, PHILLIS WHEATLEY. Providence, Oct. 26, 1775. His Excellency Gen. Washington

>Celestial choir! enthron'd in realms of light,
>Columbia's scenes of glorious toils I write.
>While freedom's cause her anxious breast alarms,
>She flashes dreadful in refulgent arms.
>See mother earth her offspring's fate bemoan,
>And nations gaze at scenes before unknown!
>See the bright beams of heaven's revolving light
>Involved in sorrows and the veil of night!
>
>The goddess comes, she moves divinely fair,
>Olive and laurel binds her golden hair:
>Wherever shines this native of the skies,
>Unnumber'd charms and recent graces rise.

Muse! bow propitious while my pen relates
How pour her armies through a thousand gates:
As when Eolus heaven's fair face deforms,
Enwrapp'd in tempest and a night of storms;
Astonish'd ocean feels the wild uproar,
The refluent surges beat the sounding shore;

Or thick as leaves in Autumn's golden reign,
Such, and so many, moves the warrior's train.
In bright array they seek the work of war,
Where high unfurl'd the ensign waves in air.
Shall I to Washington their praise recite?
Enough thou know'st them in the fields of fight.
Thee, first in place and honours,—we demand
The grace and glory of thy martial band.
Fam'd for thy valour, for thy virtues more,
Hear every tongue thy guardian aid implore!

One century scarce perform'd its destin'd round,
When Gallic powers Columbia's fury found;
And so may you, whoever dares disgrace
The land of freedom's heaven-defended race!
Fix'd are the eyes of nations on the scales,
For in their hopes Columbia's arm prevails.
Anon Britannia droops the pensive head,
While round increase the rising hills of dead.
Ah! cruel blindness to Columbia's state!
Lament thy thirst of boundless power too late.

Proceed, great chief, with virtue on thy side,
Thy ev'ry action let the goddess guide.
A crown, a mansion, and a throne that shine,
With gold unfading, WASHINGTON! be thine.

APPENDIX

[Washington's letter of response, inviting Wheatley to meet with him, followed several months later.]

Cambridge, February 28, 1776.

Mrs. Phillis: Your favour of the 26th of October did not reach my hands 'till the middle of December. Time enough, you will say, to have given an answer ere this. Granted. But a variety of important occurrences, continually interposing to distract the mind and withdraw the attention, I hope will apologize for the delay, and plead my excuse for the seeming, but not real neglect.

I thank you most sincerely for your polite notice of me, in the elegant Lines you enclosed; and however undeserving I may be of such encomium and panegyrick, the style and manner exhibit a striking proof of your great poetical Talents. In honour of which, and as a tribute justly due to you, I would have published the Poem, had I not been apprehensive, that, while I only meant to give the World this new instance of your genius, I might have incurred the imputation of Vanity. This and nothing else, determined me not to give it place in the public Prints.

If you should ever come to Cambridge, or near Head Quarters, I shall be happy to see a person so favoured by the Muses, and to whom Nature has been so liberal and beneficent in her dispensations. I am, with great Respect, etc.

About the Authors

Frederick (Rick) Spaulding received a BA in English from Harvard College and a M.Ed. from Loyola University. He taught elementary school for seven years and high school English in the Chicago Public schools for twenty-seven years. Currently he is an independent lecturer, author, and researcher. He has given over eighty lecturers in the Midwest and East Coast of the U.S.

Maurice York received a BA in literature and history from Bard College and a Masters degree in Library and Information Science from the University of Illinois. He has been writing and conducting research into American literature and history for over ten years. He is currently a librarian at North Carolina State University.

www.ingramcontent.com/pod-product-compliance
Lightning Source LLC
Chambersburg PA
CBHW031252290426
44109CB00012B/545